Roger Barrett combines the experience of a therapist with the expertise of a scholar. He is a professor of psychology at Malone College, Canton, Ohio, and a clinical psychologist with a private practice. His work includes individual and group therapy, marriage and family counseling and seminars on critical areas of mental health. He is past board president of the Suicide Prevention Center, Canton, Ohio, and is a member of the American Psychological Association and the Christian Association for Psychological Studies.

DEPRESSION

DEPRESSION
what it is and what to do about it

Roger Barrett

David C. Cook Publishing Co.
ELGIN, ILLINOIS—WESTON, ONTARIO
FULLERTON, CALIFORNIA

Published by David C. Cook Publishing Co., Elgin, IL 60120

Printed in the United States of America
Library of Congress Catalog Number: 77-79990
ISBN: 0-89191-058-1

CONTENTS

ACKNOWLEDGEMENTS

Writing a book is a bit like milking a cow—it's a joint enterprise involving a whole sequence of mutual understandings. One cannot attribute the final product to the sole efforts of either the milker or the milkee. Just so with a book like this; the final product is an amalgam of the interaction of my life and observations with that of many others who have allowed the final product to emerge.

To my wife Verna I am continuously indebted. She always lends patience and support in all my projects and shenanigans. I especially appreciate her attempts to redeem my circuitous and confused sentence structure and misuse of the English language.

To my children, Steve and Mike, who got along with less basketball and pool with Dad, and to Kirsten who put up with less tic-tac-toe and storytelling (the truly important tasks in life), and for all of them when my engrossment in writing made for more than the usual irascibleness and irritation at high noise levels, my apologies. It's hard for adults to know what's really important.

I am also deeply indebted to my clients who have allowed me to share in their lives and to learn from their experiences and trials, a kind of awareness that can never come from textbooks or the printed page. Living life vicariously with you has enriched me as a person and as a counselor. I am grateful.

To Ms. Jan Keyes I probably owe an apology as well as

thanks. She waded through my hieroglyphics of hand-written notes and made sense out of them, putting them into typewritten form when I myself couldn't read them at times.

And to Malone College I express my appreciation for a sabbatical that gave me the time to do what would not otherwise have been done.

8

PREFACE

DEPRESSION IS BEGINNING to rival schizophrenia as
the nation's number one mental health problem. According to reliable estimates, one out of every ten persons in
the U.S. may become clinically depressed at some point
in their lives. In 1970 a quarter of a million people in the
U.S. were admitted to hospitals with a diagnosis of depression, and that doesn't include those who visited a
physician, psychiatrist, psychologist, or minister but
never become a statistic through hospitalization.

Depression is a baffling disorder. It is not clear-cut and
simple as some popular authors would have us believe.
There are many theories and much conflicting research
and the answers aren't all in yet by any means. Part of the
reason for this is that depression is not a single disorder
with a single cause. What finding, cause, or cure may be
applicable to one sort of depression may have no rele-
vance for another. For that reason we will consider a
number of these different routes to depression in this
book.

Depression baffles us also because it runs counter to
basic notions about the nature of man. The notion that
man is a pleasure-seeking animal who desires to increase
pleasure and avoid pain is actually reversed in the case of
the depressed person. Basic drives such as hunger and
sex seem to vanish. Goals that motivated the person for
years are sluffed aside with abandon. We may even ig-

9

nore that supposedly innate instinct for self-preservation.

Depression not only baffles us but we often view it as too morbid to dwell on, analyze, and discuss. We ignore it, preferring happier things to talk about. Granted, a preoccupation with the dark side of human existence may be depressing in itself, but we do need to understand this side of life and to deal with it effectively. Some will need to understand it to get out of it, or understand how they got there to find their way out, or to prevent their slipping back over to the dark side again and again. That's the intention of this book. Self-discovery can be painful—but so is healing.

A warning, however: There are no fairy-tale stories here where everyone lives happily ever after, no sure-fire answers that if followed will bring happiness to one and all, no appeals to that childlike notion in all of us that the grass is greener on the other side of the fence. Speakers, authors, and workshops that promise a sure gate to the other side of the fence either squeeze life into simpler forms than it can possibly fit or overemphasize one kind of answer as *the* answer for all.

There are many gates to greener pastures. But no one can find the gate for you or push you through it. You must do that yourself with God's help. And what better help is there than that?

CHAPTER I

THE EXPERIENCE OF DEPRESSION

DEPRESSION IS a miserable, wretched experience that leaves you exhausted, unmotivated, and in deep, hopeless despair. There seems to be absolutely nowhere to turn and not one single thing you can do to escape these horrible feelings. You feel doomed, trapped, and at the end of your rope. If you've been there, you know how utterly hopeless it all seems. Misery—deep, unrelenting misery. It's awful!

Judy felt this way. She was a thirty-three-year-old mother of four. The kids, especially the little ones, needed her. She knew that, but she just couldn't get herself to get out of bed to help them. Not that she was sleeping—she really couldn't sleep. But she just couldn't get herself out of bed to face all that hassling with the children all day—day after day. She was now to the point where she would stay in bed and let the kids shift for themselves, get their own meals, their own clothes, their own snacks (she knew they were snacking all the time, lousy food for them). The house was a mess, a real mess. She hadn't done any substantial cleaning for over a month, and this last week was a total wipe out.

Tim, Judy's husband, was at the end of his rope, too. He was furious with her for giving up, or so it appeared to him. At the same time he felt sorry for her, responsible for not having helped her more with the kids or the house, being gone so much of the time, letting this depression get ahead of them without noticing it early enough. What was happening? He was utterly confused, angry at Judy, and sympathetic for her all at the same time—and worried about her, too. It just couldn't go on like this!

Guilt, guilt, guilt—both of them felt overwhelmed with a multitude of guilt feelings. Judy knew she wasn't doing for Tim and the kids what she should be doing—or for herself for that matter. She wasn't even getting out of her bed clothes and getting dressed. Nor was she going anywhere. She hadn't been out of the house now for a week. Tim was doing all the shopping and whatever cleaning up that was done. He did the dishes and he did laundry, and this just made her feel more guilty. She knew Tim hated all this being laid on him when his job was also asking a lot of him now. It was a vicious, vicious circle. The more guilty and depressed she felt, the more she couldn't get herself to do these things, and that in turn just made her *more* depressed. If only she could just go to sleep and never wake up again, this would all be over— the whole ugly mess.

But how could she think of such a thing? She was the mother of four lovely children and a husband who was trying so hard. Besides that, she claimed to be a Christian, one who is supposed to be convinced that God cares for her and loves her. But how could that be? If God cared, there wouldn't be such misery as this. "God, I hate you." And this feeling increased her guilt.

Tim struggles with guilt, too. There must be something he did, he thinks, that makes her feel so miserable. There are lots of things he can think of that he shouldn't have done or wasn't doing, but they are only little things, things that any husband might do wrong. Judy is overreacting, too sensitive. It's not all his fault. And now he's angry again. How can she do this to me? Having to call home all the time to see if the kids are alright, or if Judy has taken too many pills. How can he concentrate on work? What a mess! And now he feels guilt for feeling angry. He ought to be supporting her. She needs my support, he thinks. But how much support can you give? And why won't she try? Do something to help herself? What a mess!

Your own experiences with depression may not have been as extensive and severe as Judy's, but many people experience depression to some degree. The most mild form of depression, "the blues," are something almost everyone experiences at some points in their lives.

The Common Cold of Psychopathology

Depression has been called by mental health professionals "the common cold of psychopathology." It is experienced by so many people that it has become common to those in mental health work. It is, however, never "common" to the person experiencing it, nor is it considered mild like a cold by one caught in the throes of a depression.

Depressions come in all sizes, shapes, kinds, and degrees. They can range from very mild, transient episodes that might be labeled the "blues" to very severe forms of depression in which one's bodily processes may actually be slowed down to a life-threatening degree. Judy's depression is a moderately severe one, but it's not a psychotic depression. Some persons may become so depressed that they lose contact with reality. They may have delusions and hallucinations where they conjure up totally unrealistic and fantastic ideas or they may sense things—see, hear, feel things—that aren't there. When

13

the depression reaches these proportions it is called a psychotic depression. Most depressions don't become so severe that the persons are labeled psychotic.

There are numerous technical distinctions among these various types and kinds of depression: psychotic depression, neurotic depression, manic depression, involutional melancholia (change-of-life depression), post-partum depression, endogenous or exogenous depression. Though these distinctions and labels may be important to the therapist working with depression, they are not very meaningful to the depressed person. In fact, concern with one's diagnosis may only add to one's problems. People suffering with emotional problems are often interested in knowing what sort of label applies to them. But knowing the label often has unfortunate consequences in that people tend to overrespond to the meaning of a technical label. They impute more "craziness" to themselves than most of these labels imply. They are then convinced that they really do have a problem. They feel, once they have a label, that they really are a "mental case" or "crazy" (whatever that means) or "psychologically disabled" or "emotionally disturbed." Most of these technical labels are merely a shorthand system for communication between professionals and are not disease categories as most people tend to think of them.

Kinds of Depressions

Let's go through some of these categories just so we get a feel for some of the distinctions that exist among various types of depression. As we have already indicated, the *psychotic depression* is very severe. There is some loss of contact with reality. Delusions (irrational false beliefs) or hallucinations (sensing things not there) are usually

14

present. There may be something called "psychomotor retardation." This refers to a slowing down of bodily activity and bodily processes. The person may move so slowly or talk so quietly and slowly that it's hard to follow them. I had a professor one time in a class who was just on the back side of a severe depressive experience in which he had been hospitalized. He would move and talk so slowly that some of us in class would be sent up the wall trying to be patient enough to sit there and get the information. Incidentally, this professor was undoubtedly the best professor I've ever had. He was a brilliant and perceptive thinker, and even at the low ebb of depression he was a better stimulator of thought than most professors I've had with all their emotions intact.

Another severe depression category is termed *manic-depressive*. This originally referred to cases of mood or feeling excess that usually involved an alternation of moods from depression to euphoria and excitement and then back to a depressed mood again, etc. However, persons who don't necessarily show alternation of moods have also been classified here. This label usually implies that the person has no obvious reason for his extremes in moods. There is supposedly no outside reason to explain or account for his extremes of feeling.

The *neurotic depression* is a more mild form of depression. The person experiences no loss of contact with reality. He usually continues to function in his life tasks, but only with great difficulty. He suffers from an acute loss of self-esteem and has problems motivating himself.

Involutional melancholia (now that's a mouthful) refers to the stage of life for both men and women when they go through physiological changes that make it less likely that they will be able to reproduce. This is frequently an agitated depression, i.e., rather than being slowed down the person is highly agitated and anxious. He is likely to

15

be very restless and tense. Hypochondriacal preoccupation is frequent. (That simply means that the person has aches and pains that they focus on and are highly concerned about.) They frequently doubt their competency. They often feel as though they are worthless and can't accomplish anything.

Post-partum depression refers to a continuing depressed mood experienced by a woman following child birth. It usually doesn't last long, but the problem is that at this very time she is much needed by the newborn child.

One very interesting depression has been called *"success depression."* This is not a technical category, but happens frequently enough to be viewed as a syndrome of its own. It is interesting because it appears to be a paradox. It appears to occur following the successful accomplishment of a long term goal where the individual has put in long periods of time and disciplined effort. Earning a degree in a long term program like an M.D. or Ph.D. is an example of this. Once achieved you'd expect absolute euphoria and utter bliss rather than depression, but for some people the period immediately following the accomplishment of this long sought after goal is followed by a down period of emptiness and depression. It also can occur for the person who has worked for years to get to the top or to some particular position, or to acquire wealth, affluence or financial security.

It all seems so baffling. Why would anyone feel blue for "arriving"? Actually it can be explained in part by the old proverb "the grass is always greener on the other side of the fence." Once we get to the other side of the fence, it seems the grass is never quite as different as it had appeared from our previous perspective. And the weeds—they are always there! (But you frequently have to get up close to see them clearly.) The famous nihilistic philosopher Nietzsche spoke of the "melancholia of ev-

16

erything completed." I think this suggests that the attaining of goals always leaves us with a loss of some kind, a vacuum that needs to be filled. That may also account to some degree for this so-called "success depression."

Sometimes a distinction is made between *endogenous* or *exogenous* depression. *Endogenous* means internally caused or originating within the body, and *exogenous* means externally or environmentally caused or originating outside the body. Sometimes the word *reactive* is used with similar meaning to exogenous. Since it is often difficult to determine whether a depression is directly attributable to outside events or inside factors, this distinction can be somewhat arbitrary. As a result, the terms endogenous and exogenous are used by some practitioners to refer to different patterns of symptoms in depression.

It may be that problems such as alcoholism and some forms of obesity are actually forms of depression. Mental health professionals sometimes speak of "masked depression," which means that the usual symptoms of depression may be covered up by other kinds of behaviors. Excessive drinking is a good example. The individual may resort to drinking to cope with his bad feelings. An outsider may not see the depressed symptoms, but only the excessive drinking behavior. Or someone else may resort to excessive eating when down or blue. When these ways of coping with bad feelings become habitual, we may not see the depression so much as the habitual behavior. These, of course, will only temporarily mask the depression, and in the long run they become part of a vicious cycle that will only make the depression worse.

Grief or *bereavement,* the sad feelings we have following the loss of a loved one, are actually forms of depression. We just don't classify these feelings as disordered be-

17

havior because it's normal to have such feelings. It is even considered *healthy* to experience these feelings, and to be in touch with these feelings when we have experienced such a loss. But what we may experience in grief or bereavement may be identical to the experience and symptoms of a depression. If grief reactions tend to be unduly prolonged or of extreme severity, they may become what we call *reactive depression*. Many persons who go through divorce also experience a grief reaction. In this case it tends not to be called grief, but is more likely to be classified as depression. That all seems very arbitrary to me. I'm not at all sure that the loss of a loved one however it occurs may not involve some form of grief and bereavement and that that is really quite normal.

In sum, we can see that depressed people and depressed experiences vary both in quantity and quality. Two persons, both of whom are experiencing depression, may have as many things different about their experience as similar. Not only are there multiple forms of expression of depression, but there are also many different causes of depression (as we shall describe in detail at a later point in the book). Therefore, be careful not to apply everything that you read in this book to either yourself (if you experience depression) or to an individual you know who is depressed. Depression is much too complex to make easy individual application. What may be true for one depressed person may not in any way apply to another equally depressed person.

Empty, Anxious, Angry, and Sickness Depressions

I have come across one attempt to distinguish between kinds of depression that I think is simple to understand and helpful. One research study attempted to see if there were statistically identifiable differences in the experiences of depression in a group of depressed individuals. The results helped the researchers classify four types which they called: 1) Empty Depression; 2) Anxious Depression; 3) Hypochondriacal Depression; and 4) Angry Depression.

The Empty Depressives have feelings of helplessness and low self-esteem. They are apathetic with slower speech, thought, and motor movement. There is a kind of "given up" quality to them.

The Anxious Depressive also experiences low self-esteem and helplessness but also feels an overwhelming anxiety. This person is agitated and a clinging-dependent type in his relations with others. Whereas the Empty Depressive may withdraw from others and prefer isolation, the Anxious Depressive is more likely to be involved with other people and to make demands on them.

The third type, the Hypochondriacal Depressive, complains not so much of bad feelings as of bodily complaints of one kind or another and is apt to express these feelings in persistent and often exaggerated physical complaints. It is almost as if these types channel their depression into their bodies. As with the Anxious Depressive, the Hypochondriacal may be rather demanding in his relationships with others.

The Angry Depressive, of course, expresses those bad feelings in anger at others and/or himself. He may be quite provocative, and unhappiness and gloom dominate his conversation.

I have found these four categories of depression helpful in working with depressed persons, and they have suggested ways of aiding people in coping with their depression as well as in understanding it and its possible causes. Therefore I'll refer to these four types frequently in the chapters that follow.

19

Common Characteristics of Depression

In spite of the distinctions we've made between the different kinds and types of depression, there are many experiences and symptoms that most depressed people have in common. Let's look at these for a moment.

Sadness is the most obvious characteristic of depression. Depressed persons feel unhappy and miserable. They seem unable to enjoy anything, even things they enjoyed greatly before. Attempts by others to bouy them up usually fail. They lose their sense of humor, and cry frequently, often without provocation. That in itself is disconcerting to them. "Why do I cry all the time? And for what reason?" Sometimes the weeping will seem impossible to stop, and they cry so much they become exhausted. The opposite may also be true—they seem totally unable to cry. When this is the case, they feel as if they wish they could cry but just aren't able.

Depression is also characterized by lots of bad feelings for the self. Depressed people feel absolutely and completely worthless. Their self-esteem is virtually non-existent. Their confidence is gone. As a result it's harder for them to try things, to take on tasks, to go to social events, meet people or even go to work. They may feel totally incompetent and inefficient. Nor will reminders of past accomplishments or talents restore this confidence or self-esteem.

I once worked with a young man who was the epitome of achievement and success for his age level. He was a star athlete in both basketball and baseball, a straight A student, and a student council leader. I also found that he was highly respected by both faculty and students alike. He was unusually handsome with the girls agog over him. Yet, in spite of all this, he struggled with these very feelings of depression we are speaking about—

worthlessness, inadequacy, ineptness, and ineffective-ness. It came home to me as a new counselor how totally incongruent and utterly unrealistic these feelings can be. The feelings of the person and reality of his life may be on totally different wavelengths. This disparity between reality and the feelings may baffle those around de-pressed persons. It seems so impossible that they should be feeling this way, given their assets and accomplish-ments.

Loss of interest is pervasive for most depressed per-sons. Nothing seems to motivate them. Things that pre-viously turned them on may now only irritate them. Even basic motivators such as food or sex lack appeal for them. Sexual activity may be not only reduced but eliminated. (That, too, will create guilt feelings for the depressed individual and anger or frustration in the spouse.) They typically lose interest in church activities and other social involvements.

Part of this loss of interest in the social domain is the desire to hide, to stay away from others, to withdraw into oneself. Frequently depressed people will sever all social ties and responsibilities. They will ask to be removed from committees, being church organist, drop out of club membership, etc. Or they just stop attending. They may even try to quit their jobs or leave a marriage. I remember one young man who was unusually active and involved. His job was a highly social one in which he was constantly involved with people. Not only did he quit his job, but he resigned from a second job he had as a youth leader in a church, resigned from a board, quit a softball team, gave up his girl friend, quit attending church, and just withdrew into himself—completely and utterly alone.

Often depressed persons can't sleep. They may have difficulty getting to sleep in the first place, or they wake up in the middle of the night and can't get back to sleep. Or the opposite problem may exist. They may escape into a world of sleep and stay in bed most of the day, sleeping for fourteen, fifteen hours at a time. Or they may be totally unable to get up even though they've slept well.

Loss of appetite is also common. Or, again, the opposite—they may eat compulsively at depressed times—a kind of escape into food. Loss of appetite frequently results in extreme and rapid weight loss. This is a major concern to the clinician who must consult a physician to watch the effects of this loss of appetite and weight. Energy loss, which is already a problem, is aggravated by the lack of proper nutrition. Another of the vicious circles of depression comes into play.

Feelings of guilt often accompany depression. In one chapter in this book, we will focus on the relationship between guilt and depression in some depth, especially as it involves the Christian faith, so we will forego any extensive discussion here. Let us say here that both the Christian and the non-Christian alike experience self-blame and guilt related to depression, and the guilt they feel may or may not be realistic or reasonable. One may feel guilty for not cleaning an already spotless house as well as feeling guilty for having violated an ordinance of God. Guilt feelings range from the ridiculous to the essential in depressions.

Feelings of inefficiency are another usual feature of depression. The depressed person often feels that, e.g., on his job he just does not measure up and simply can't do his job. Depressives often report that they can't think and solve problems. Recent research evidence, however, suggests that this is misleading. Intellectual impairment or deficit has *not* been found in research studies. However, this is the *feeling* that most, if not all, depressives

22

seem to experience, so much so that they may feel they must quit their job, e.g., as they are just not being fair to their employer. Many times hearing from employers I have found that they are not at all unhappy with the depressed person's work. They are, in fact, quite pleased with the employee and view them as one of their more conscientious workers. If there is any problem it is that they are too conscientious or overly precise in their work—not that they are inefficient.

Well, now that we have discussed the kinds of depression that exist as well as the symptoms found to be common in most depressions, let us go on to see what brings on depression.

CHAPTER II

WHAT BROUGHT THIS DEPRESSION ON?

LOUISE WAS VERY TIGHT and nervous and a bit confused when she came into the office. I could see she was startled by the "unmedical" looking nature of the setting—the shag rug, the couch, the over-stuffed chairs, the plants. She made some comment to the effect that this looked more like a living room than a doctor's office. It does and I like that.

Her story came out slowly. Louise wasn't sure she was in the right place. She needed to test me out a bit at first, but soon it started coming. She was depressed—and scared by it. She was seventy-two years old, living alone in her small house, and had never married. There was a young man once, but it hadn't worked out. She and her parents (mostly her parents, I surmise) thought he should go to college, but it wasn't in his plans and so she had told him, "no, she couldn't marry him." Now forty-eight years later she wasn't sure that had been right. Besides, he had done just fine without a college education. And why should this be so important now, at this time? Why was she reliving it in her mind over and over? And all kinds of other mistakes from the past—why were they all coming back to haunt her?

Her hands trembled as she talked. Soon the tears came, and that was sort of embarrassing. The Kleenex box was on the end table. I handed it to her; that was kind of reassuring. She guessed I was "used to people crying." Maybe then it wasn't so bad. People her age, she informed me, didn't go in for this psychology business so easily like the young ones seem to be doing. So this was difficult, like an admission of not being able to handle your own affairs.

You couldn't help but like Louise. She was a beautiful person with a lot of integrity, independence of spirit, and guts. It isn't easy for her generation to go for help or to admit they haven't got it all together, but her depression was becoming an increasingly downward spiral for her. She could feel it, each day worse than the previous one, and she had to do something. So here she was.

What had caused this, she wondered. She couldn't put her finger on anything that would really explain it. That in itself was a bit scary. As we inquired together what was currently going on in her life and the nature of her life-style it came out that she had just recently lost her living partner of the last twenty-three years. This partner, recently turned eighty, had become senile and had to be put in a convalescent home in a town 200 miles away where "her people" lived. Then, too, a good friend and neighbor had died recently. Their gardens adjoined, and there had been lots of good companionship there for many years.

Loss—Louise had suffered significant reduction in the relationships that had made her life meaningful. And, as we shall soon see, loss, particularly of intimates, as well as losses in general are a major precipitating cause of depression.

But many seventy-year-olds lose their partners and friends. Losses are all around you at that age, and they don't all become depressed—saddened certainly, but not depressed.

25

Predisposing and/or Precipitating?

This brings up one of the most critical distinctions to be made in the area of emotional breakdown in general and depression in particular. That is the distinction between predisposing and precipitating factors. Almost always current happenings trigger off the disorder which has been set up from events in the past. You can't really pull them apart or view them separately. Unfortunately both the depressed person and those around him often grab for the explanation that some triggering event was sufficient in itself to explain the depression. And if it is just a "straw" that's found, it all becomes so baffling—and even more depressing.

"The straw that broke the camel's back" is a good illustration for us here. The camel's broken back can be explained by a number of factors. Maybe we don't have a very strong camel in the first place. He has a weak back. Or maybe he just hasn't worked out with heavy loads enough. (Many people haven't experienced enough stress in appropriate amounts in younger years to have learned how to cope with it.) The camel's back is strong enough all right, but he just hasn't worked out enough to build up the supporting muscles. Or maybe it was the suddenness of the additional weight being added—too much all at once. He could have handled it had the load been added more gradually. Or maybe he's carrying around such a heavy load all the time that he is constantly exhausted. (Many people constantly carry heavy loads of adverse past experiences around with them, which in turn keeps them emotionally run down.)

We have something in clinical psychology we call frustration or stress tolerance level. Individuals do not have the same tolerance level in coping with stress. The same adverse event may be a precipitating or triggering event

26

for emotional problems or depression for one individual and no problem at all to another person whose stress tolerance level is higher. Our ability to tolerate stress relates to what we call the "predisposing" factors.

This brings up a critical dimension I wish we could all get ahold of. It is the idea that we can't judge a person's mental health and well-being simply because he has had emotional problems or an emotional breakdown. He may actually be quite healthy mentally, i.e., he may have a fairly high stress tolerance level, but stress for him just got to be too much. The person who has experienced an emotional breakdown may be healthier than either you or I who haven't had such an experience. It's just that he has experienced more stress than we have.

Maybe if we diagram this concept it would be helpful.

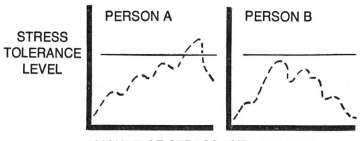

A and B refer to two people who have similar stress tolerance levels. The straight line indicates their level of stress tolerance. The hatched line indicates the amount of stress they have experienced. At the point that the amount of stress we experience is higher than our stress tolerance level, we will experience some sort of emotional breakdown. As you can see, Person A has experienced more stress at one point in time than has Person B. (Even

27

though Person B has been close to that point on two occasions, it never crossed the point of his ability to cope with it.)

Unfortunately, and with some pharisaical disdain, someone will point to Person A and say, "He's emotionally weak" or "he has mental problems." They won't say the same about Person B, even though A and B are really of equal emotional stability.

It is even possible that someone with a lower stress tolerance level ("weak emotionally") may not experience emotional disorder or breakdown when a much stronger person may *because* he has experienced much more stress.

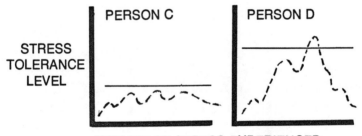

Person C has less good mental health or emotional stability than Person D. But he never experiences more stress than he can cope with. Person D has considerable more ability to cope with stress by comparison to Person C, but he has also far more severe and stressful events and problems, and they have, on one occasion, exceeded his ability to handle them.

If we can really get hold of this concept, it can save us from simplistic and critical judgments of those around us. It certainly is helpful to me as a therapist. I do not assume in any way that I as a therapist am a "strong person," emotionally speaking, working with people with "weak emotions." Not at all. The person so desperate in my counseling office may have experienced far more grief, stress, and problems than I have ever even come close to.

Characteristic Stress Factors in Depression

Because both precipitating and predisposing factors make up a depressive experience, let's take a look at each of them separately. We will call the precipitating or triggering factors the stress factors. Psychologists have identified for us certain stresses that seem to trigger depressive episodes. Let's take a look at these.

For men the events that seem most often associated with the onset of depression are events like financial reversals, failures in vocational identity (such as failure to make a promotion or achieve some vocational goal), and failing physical powers of one kind or another.

The triggering events for women differ. The major factors appear to be such events as attacks on her femininity (e.g., a mastectomy or hysterectomy). Even more significant is the feeling (or reality) of being abandoned by important men in her life such as her father or husband. The loss of children either through accident or the inevitable separation of child from parent through the child's growing up and away from mother may trigger depression. Trouble of one kind or another in the home often triggers off depression in females.

Notice how different these stress factors are for men and women and how much the factors relate to male and female roles in our society. For both sexes the critical factors precipitating the onset of depression seem to relate to their identities. For the man the identity is that of provider and wage-earner and for the female it appears to be the identity of homemaker and caretaker of the home. No doubt as the roles of males and females change in our society the precipitating factors making for depression will also change. However, the underlying factor I believe will remain the same, i.e., from whatever a person derives his identity, that is, those features that determine *who he is* will be the features, which, when lost, can result in triggering depression.

All the above precipitating factors involve the *sense of worth* an individual has of himself. Apparently the female's sense of worth is tied very closely to her appearance and her relationship to her family members, whereas a man's sense of worth is more closely tied to his work and his physical prowess. We might question whether this *should* be true for the Christian especially. Should these identities mean so much to us that their loss can have devastating effect on our emotional well-being? The loss or removal of *anything* we overvalue in terms of our security can trigger depression. Are these the areas of life in which the Christian is to place his security? I doubt it.

Loss

Did you notice how much the idea of *loss* was involved in the precipitating factors mentioned—loss of a spouse or child, loss of a promotion, loss of physical powers, loss of attractiveness, etc.? In many if not most depressions there is a personal loss of some kind involved. If not an actual loss, it may involve *fears of loss*. Some people, because of their excessive dependency (a topic to which we will devote an entire chapter later on), dwell on and become preoccupied with imagined possible losses and as a result precipitate depressive feelings and even episodes

30

in themselves. Because their security depends on some person or thing external to their own person or relation to God, they constantly feel jeopardized by the possibility of losing that person or object.

Again, the loss or removal of *anything* we overvalue in terms of our security can precipitate depression. If sense of worth depends on money or social position, or appearance, or athletic skill, or job or reputation, or drugs, or community standing, or church office, or singing voice, or any of the myriad of things into which we can invest our self-esteem, to that extent we will be threatened by its loss.

The Old Testament story of Job portrays in great detail the principal role that loss (whether real or imagined) plays in triggering depression. Poor Job. He lost about everything one could possibly lose. He lost all his wealth as well as his means of livelihood. He lost his servants. He even lost his children. Finally he lost his physical health and well-being. And as a result of this horrendous calamity, Job experienced the depths of depression. Listen to these complaints of Job:

> "Let the day perish wherein I was born, and the night which said, 'A manchild is conceived.' Let that day be darkness!"
> "Why did I not die at birth, come forth from the womb and expire?"
> "Why is light given to him that is in misery, and life to the bitter in soul, who long for death, but it comes not, and dig for it more than for hid treasures."
> "For my sighing comes as my bread, and my groanings are poured out like water."
> "In truth I have no help in me, and any resource is driven from me."
> " . . . so I am allotted months of emptiness, and nights of misery are apportioned to me. When I lie down I say, 'When shall I arise?' But the night is long, and I am full of tossing till the dawn."

"My face is red with weeping, and on my eyelids is deep darkness."
"If I say to the pit, 'You are my father,' and to the worm, 'My mother,' or 'My sister,' where then is my hope?"

In chapter one we spoke of a "success depression." One may well ask what is the loss here? If one has arrived at that new M.D. degree or finally has made it to that top executive position, or that long-sought-for foreman's job—what loss could there possibly be? If you stop to think of it even here there is a loss—a loss of goals. One may have arrived at a point from which he has no further goal or direction. He is without a rudder until he formulates a new direction or goal for himself. Goals provide us direction.

We also spoke of *grief* or *bereavement* in chapter one as a kind of depression, a normal depression in which we've lost a loved one, someone for whom one cared deeply. As we said then, depression is a normal emotional reaction to such a personal loss.

Without doubt the number one loss that precipitates depression in the majority of depressed clients that I see is the loss of a spouse through divorce, unfaithfulness, or indifference. Again and again the story repeats itself with little variance. They became increasingly aware that their spouse was losing interest. He or she was staying away more. Frequency of sexual intercourse and affectionate displays decreased. The spouse became surly, finding fault, full of criticism, unable to say one nice word. Communication about problems, about anything, became non-existent. Then the explosions, the blow-ups. In these blow-ups they are told that the marriage never has been good, the spouse claims to have been unhappy with the marriage for years (though this may never have been indicated or even implied in all the years before). And of course if we believe, as Christians do, that man is a sinner, then marriage is a relation of two imperfect people in an imperfect relationship, and one can *always* find ingredients that make criticism warranted. So the criticisms are not without basis. But that's all there is at these times. They can't seem to see any of the positive attributes of the mate or the relationship.

Eventually the disgruntled spouse gives the "I don't love you anymore and maybe never did" speech. Up to this point the other mate has become very anxious and even agitated, but now depression enters. If the wayward spouse is a female, she now "can't stand to be touched" at all by her husband. Or if the disgruntled one is the husband, he just appears to have little or no sexual interest to speak of. Then the suspicions set in, and so it goes.

When the bewildered spouse finally seeks professional help, things are already far too advanced. There is often a weight loss. They have just had no appetite at all through all this. Tears come easily at almost any time, and at times they don't feel they can stop crying.

This is how it was for Lois. She knew something was wrong, but because she was so busy with the kids, three pre-schoolers and one in second, it hadn't really dawned on her what was happening. Yes, he was saying he had to go to the office in the evening more and more, and when he did come home he was so tired he wasn't really interested in sex. But that really hadn't bothered Judy. She had always been so tired she hadn't been that enthusiastic about sex in the evenings anyway. Once the twins were in bed and Debbie and Rex were down she was exhausted, and it was actually a kind of relief not to have him hassling her at that time for a physical relationship. But now, looking back, it appeared ominous.

And now he snapped at her and the kids or blew up about something whenever he was at home. Even the kids were beginning to ask, "What's wrong with Daddy?" They had always been so eager to have him home. He was fun, and they liked the change of pace from being with Mom all day, but now they avoided him when he was there.

And why all the cologne smell for evenings at the office? And those times where she came into the bedroom and he'd almost slam the phone down, so obviously guilty-like. Then there was that time his boss called to ask where he was when he'd told her the two of them were supposed to complete this proposal that Saturday.

Then the accusations, frantic and angry, Lois hated herself for how she had handled that. He denied everything, and told her it was all in her head, that she was getting paranoid. She wondered, perhaps she really was losing touch at times. Where was truth? What really was happening? Lois was confused, anxious and very highly agitated. She couldn't sleep. She'd wake up worrying about it all. She couldn't eat. Food had no appeal. When she finally came to seek help she had lost twenty pounds in six weeks, and she didn't have that much to lose to begin with.

Then came that horrible Tuesday evening and all night long of accusations and denials ending up with that cruel listing of all her bad traits and how long he had been unhappy. Finally he added that he guessed he never had loved her—the kids, yes, but not her. For the last three years it had been increasingly difficult to even tolerate her. Yes, there was someone else, but they were just friends, that's all. He had "wanted more," but hadn't "done anything." And it wasn't any attraction to this other "party" that had made him unhappy. He'd been unhappy long before he had even met her. No, he wouldn't tell her who this was. And if Lois pushed it, he'd just leave.

Could they talk to the pastor or someone? Absolutely not! After all, it wasn't as if he were involved with someone. If only Lois had known then how involved he was. And now that she finally did know, and knew who this other woman was as well, all Lois' anger was turned on her. She had just flagrantly pursued John in spite of the fact she knew he was married and had children, and Lois had heard that she'd done this before. It was as though if Lois could get her anger totally focused on this wretched Jezebel, she wouldn't be so angry at John. Feelings of love and hate for John were so mixed it was ripping her apart. Memories of all those good times, the closeness, the warmth, the honest-to-goodness togetherness all mixed together with the current hatred and anger and hurt. It was all so utterly exhausting and *depressing*. There was no doubt about it—Lois was depressed.

Loss, loss of spouse, especially through unfaithfulness and the frequent alienation associated with divorce is much worse emotionally than the loss of spouse through death. Both are depressing experiences, but the former carries with it such a complex and chaotic set of feelings that it has a much greater potential for triggering depression.

Chronic Stress

Sometimes there has been no critical event or loss that triggers the depression. Instead a long series of stresses or simply chronic stress finally topples the person's emotional well-being and depression enters.

If a person is constantly anxious and fearful and he keeps these fears and anxieties around long enough, he can eventually use up all his energy, exhaust himself emotionally and physically, and become depressed. If stress is severe enough and applied long enough, the hormonal reserves of the body become depleted. This results in fatigue and eventually exhaustion. The feeling side of this physical experience is depression.

A strong argument against allowing ourselves to be uptight, tense, nervous, anxious all the time is just this. Eventually it catches up with us, and we leave ourselves open to the risk of depression. I myself am one of these busy, busy, impatient sorts. I like to have a lot of things going. As a result, I frequently overcommit myself, especially to outside speaking engagements. Then there's always the anxiety of preparation as well as delivery. (I hope I never lose that.) And if I get too many in a row together with my other commitments, I find myself running here and there and never slowing down. Even though I enjoy the opportunities to speak, I also know it keeps my anxiety level high. If I don't control my schedule, I get exhausted and down. It's just not worth the risk. One needs to pace himself for the future.

Those of you who coddle fears and anxieties also need to beware. Living on a constant diet of fears of what the future may bring, or worries about what could happen eventually, if severe enough, can exhaust you to the point where you can't resist depression. The Bible admonition, "Have no anxiety about anything" (Phil. 4:6) is good psychological advice—demanding, but good. Incidentally, that passage also goes on to suggest to us a method for coping with those anxieties.

Predisposers to Depression

Now that we have considered the precipitating factors that may trigger depression, let us look at the predisposing factors, those long-standing personality characteristics that set us up so that depression can be triggered. After all, not everyone who loses a spouse becomes depressed. Not everyone who experiences a financial reversal gets depressed. Not everyone who fails to get a desired promotion falls victim to depression. And very few individuals who achieve success find depression on the back side.

What's the difference? Why some and not others? Even when the triggering events, the immediate stress, is similar or at times identical?

Back to our by now somewhat overburdened camel. The straw that breaks the camel's back we said is not sufficient in itself to explain the event. Just so with the precipitating events that we have been discussing. There must be additional ingredients or else everyone would be depressed in those same stressful circumstances.

Not every young mother gets depressed over the demands of diapers, bottles, spilt milk, sibling hassles, and crying, but Jo Anne did. Her three children were nine months, two, and four. When Jo Anne came into the office, she couldn't stop crying, really sobbing. And her complaint was just that—she cried all the time at home and sometimes couldn't stop. "I can't stand to see the kids get up in the morning. I don't mean I don't love them. I love them dearly. But they drive me up the wall." And she sobbed some more. "And by the time the evening comes I am so tired I can hardly move." She spent a lot of time in bed. "If I go out shopping without the kids I hate to come back. And that's horrible. No mother should feel like that. I can't stand to be alone, and I get all upset if I can't get to my husband when I'm like this."

There is no question, caring for three small children in a small house is very demanding—emotionally and physically. But few harried young mothers ever get as harried and depressed as Jo Anne. She was to the point where it was almost impossible to take care of her own children.

Later in our interviews it came out that this uncontrolled crying wasn't new. At one point she said, "I cried all the way through high school, and through two pregnancies." They had to live in even smaller quarters, a trailer, while they attended school. Married young, partly to escape a demanding mother, life had been tough for Jo Anne. As we investigated we found a lot of personality characteristics in Jo Anne, long before babies arrived on the scene, that made depression a possibility, even a likelihood.

A number of psychological studies have attempted to find out what kind of personality characteristics are common to persons who eventually become depressed. These studies have taken groups of depressed patients (usually hospitalized) and given them personality tests or investigated their histories for personality characteristics that existed *before* they become depressed. This is a very difficult kind of research (getting retroactive data), and so the results are not considered especially trustworthy by psychologists. But what has at least been suggested by these studies is very interesting, and I would like to sum them up for you.

One study suggested that depressed persons had been perfectionists who led narrow lives filled with exaggerated concern for being on time, doing the right thing, and always meeting their responsibilities. Another characteristic was that they had limited capacity for relaxation and emotional expression, i.e., they kept their emotions under tight constraint. It was also interestingly found that these individuals were highly regarded by others as they could always be relied on. But they were also considered to be rather rigid and highly moralistic.

Another study suggested that the personality of the eventually depressed person was characterized by an overriding need to gain the approval of others first, as well as slavish sensitivity to do's and don'ts, shoulds and shouldn'ts. Their lives were dominated by strict order and rules. They seemed to have a life-style devoted to fulfilling their sense of order and avoiding risk.

Yet another study suggested that these individuals were over-conscientious, striving, and conforming persons who had very high needs to achieve. They had difficulty accepting contradictory facets in other people. They tended to operate on an all-or-none basis, i.e., things are either good or bad, desirable or objectionable.

Another study found that depressed personalities were marked by high needs for order, high needs to have others care for them and attend to their needs. They did not like change or to assume positions of dominance.

I don't know your reaction to these findings, but mine was amazement and disbelief, at least at first glance. Many of these characteristics were ingrained into me in my evangelical Christian background as a child and youth as high virtues, personality characteristics to be highly desired and sought after in both myself and others. If they can bring on depression, they can hardly be virtues, can they? Being on time, being conscientious, always meeting responsibilities, concern for doing the right thing, being the kind of person others can rely on, having a set of rules to live by, having things done properly and in order—these are the marks of what a Christian *should* be like, are they not? And these people sound pretty normal, too. And all this, these virtues, are the seedbed for depression? How can it be? Is it possible to have too much of a good thing?

Perfectionism

The major part of this book is an attempt to deal with this problem. Many observations about this seeming dilemma will be coming throughout the chapters that fol-

low. Let us for the moment, however, make some observations about these seemingly virtuous strands running
through these studies. One obvious strand is that these
are people who never seem to measure up to their own
expectations of themselves, or what they believe are
other people's expectations of them. Perfectionism permeates the predisposing characteristics in these studies.
Now perfectionism can be, in fact, *is* a most heavy cross to
bear. If perfectionism is the goal, one of course never
arrives, you can never accept yourself. You are always
falling short, always inadequate.

But doesn't Christianity require no less of us? "You,
therefore, must be perfect, as your heavenly Father is
perfect" (Matt. 5:48). Certainly it is true that as Christians we have high goals set out for us. But that does not
mean high goals in absolutely everything that we do.
Every so often I have heard some speaker make the
statement that a Christian is to strive for excellence in
"anything that he turns his hand to." That, quite frankly,
bugs me. For if you carry it to its logical extreme it
becomes an impossibility. You can't be perfect or excel in
everything. You can't even do your best in everything.
This notion also does not take into account the fact that
we all are given different gifts.

Let me illustrate the problem. Cathy has very high
goals for the appearance of her home. Not only is the
decor impressive, but the house is spotless. Add to that
the fact that Cathy has made her home beautiful and
pleasant not at very great financial cost, but through her
own creativity and diligence. That has meant lots of time
and effort, so much, in fact, that the kids have come out
on the short end of Cathy's time and attention. Oh, she's
been an adequate mother by most standards, but she has
seldom had time to read to them and *never* any time to
play with them. At times she has been downright grumpy

and mean when the kids have interfered with her attempts to reach her standards of "what a house should be like."

What we are suggesting is, of course, quite obvious. The goal is not perfection in everything that we do. In fact, the Bible exegetes suggest to us this passage, "Be ye perfect . . ." really has reference not to what our English word perfection means at all, but rather to the concept of completion or fulfillment. And psychologically that is so much more meaningful as well as tons less burdensome than perfectionistic demands for all areas of my being. For Cathy it may suggest that she tone down a bit on all this "nice home" obsession and let that bedroom go without those "just right" curtains for awhile longer so that she can frolic with the kids. "They are only young once" is cheap advice I suppose, but it's not cheap in God's economy of time. To be the "complete" mother and housewife is what Scripture requests of Cathy. And that's plenty! Without having to be perfect in everything.

Orderliness

Another quality running through those studies that at first impression sounds virtuous, but with further reflection can be seen to be of only dubious value, is the concern for orderliness. "On time," "can always be relied on," "having things just so"—these characteristics are certainly desirable (a lot of us could do with a lot more here), but they can be overdone or done for the wrong reasons. Many of these people have such an extremely high need for order because of a basic underlying insecurity they feel inside. And so as a result they attempt to cope with this insecurity and anxiety by structuring and ordering every thing according to rigid patterns. They can't stand to have these orders and routines upset.

41

There is no question that the affairs and tasks of life should be done "decently and in order," but orderliness which has calcified into rigidity is not what God asks.

Law and Order Types

Another seeming virtue that runs through these studies characterizing the personality of the depressed person is that of standards—he is the kind of individual who follows the rules, who meets the regulations. But note a kind of compulsiveness to this rules and regulations orientation that suggests what may be at stake here. It is *slavish* sensitivity to do's and don'ts, shoulds and shouldn'ts. This individual is *driven* to be good. He is ridden by a sense of duty and obedience. He is good, but it is a goodness out of fear. That's why it is so compulsive.

Many children are good out of fear of punishment or because they have a strong authoritarian parent of whom they are afraid. They are obedient, not because they really want to be that way, but because they are scared not to be. The Christian is a person who subscribes to the rules he believes God has suggested for us because he had freely chosen them as the best way to result in his own and other's well being. It is not slavish but freely chosen. There is a freedom and autonomy to it all that is anything but authoritarian, rigid, and compulsive. Not slaves, but free, self-choosing agents. Moral, yes, but not moralistic.

These observations that we have made about the seeming virtues of the long-term personality characteristics of the depressed individual and their relationship to the Christian faith deserve more thoughtful attention, so we will come back to these issues again.

CHAPTER III

CHILDHOOD DETERMINANTS
OF DEPRESSION

IN THE PREVIOUS CHAPTER we noted the predisposing or long term personality characteristics that have been found in many depressed persons. Now comes the question—what made them like that? Did something in their early life bring about these drives for perfectionism and orderliness; this slavish sensitivity to rules and regulations? Or did these characteristics just come on with the depression? Or are these personality features a matter of temperament and genetics? The next question then is, what is there, if anything, that is characteristic about the childhood of these people?

We want to investigate these possible childhood contributions to depression for at least two reasons. One is so that those of you who struggle with depression or live with someone who does may gain some understanding of how some of these things started. But even more important, I think, is for parents to gain some understanding of what they can do to avoid "setting up" children as candidates for depression.

Achievement

Frequently in studying the childhood of depressives, we find they have been pushed to achieve. They have been pushed quite hard by their parents to *measure up*. Also it appears that their parents have pressured them to *conform*. One study suggests that not only have parents pushed them to conform and achieve, but that these children have reacted to these demands by adopting the values of their parents and faithfully, dutifully, and desperately trying to meet the demands of their parents. They go along with the regime as good boys and girls.

Several studies suggest that the families of depressed persons show a high degree of striving for prestige and that (for various reasons) the children of these families become an instrument of these needs. The child becomes an instrument of social striving. By competing and excelling he secures his parents' attention and approval, but not if he doesn't. There comes a kind of unconscious need for him to win prestige for the family. One study suggests that the parents are working to improve the family's social acceptability and that the children are expected to conform to a high standard of behavior based primarily on what the neighbors or the parents' social set expect.

We have all seen parents who can talk of nothing but the athletic, social, or academic success of their children and who push their children into one competitive activity after another. They have an inordinate degree of concern about social approval, and social approval is (in their minds) gained by successful competition and achievement. Achievement or excellence is determined by "doing better than others" (which of course is an endless quest as there is always someone in this world left to beat out).

It is easy to see where perfectionism can get started in such an environment. A child raised in this kind of home will always feel he needs to do better, that his parents' approval is contingent on his winning, "doing better than," "beating out," or even putting others down. He becomes a highly competitive person *whether he wins or not.*

This also cultivates the seedbed for envy. (And as we shall see later, envy is a frequent problem for depressed persons.) This is especially true if the child competes somewhat unsuccessfully, but knows that his worth and value are at stake in his eyes and in the eyes of his parents. Oh, parents like this seldom indicate their dissatisfaction with unsuccessful competition or lower than expected achievement directly, but their dissatisfaction is quickly perceived by the child or youth. (I've found that parents like this are very quick to inform you—even before you ask—that they accept and appreciate Johnny regardless, but their enthusiasm and preoccupation for his success betray them.)

I had a client once, an eager Christian woman and mother who had struggled periodically in her life with depression. Whenever she came in for a session, she rehearsed endlessly the accomplishments of her children, largely in the athletic and academic areas. I also knew privately some of her friends and had heard from them that she could talk of nothing else. Though the father didn't talk about it so much, it was obvious that achievement and success were paramount for him. He had finally become president of a company, but that still didn't constitute arrival for him and his long work hours kept increasing.

Unfortunately, one of the children, a teenage daughter, didn't either achieve or conform to the expectations that had so dominated their lives. The daughter eventually gave up—why try if no matter how hard you try it isn't enough. She also rebelled. This, of course, was disastrous for this mother, for her own preoccupation with her children's success was really a vicarious attempt to deal with her own deep insecurities and failure to measure up. What would people say? Anger and concern for her daughter dominated Mother's thinking—anger because she had betrayed the family and their goals and standards, and yet concern that her daughter not get permanently hurt by her waywardness.

Interestingly enough, and quite predictable, the daughter now struggles with depression. The problem, of course, is that the child internalizes these standards of achievement and competitiveness and sooner or later adopts his parents' expectations for himself. As adults we find that depressed people almost always score higher than most on both "need" for achievement and "valuing" of achievement. It remains very, very important, *too* important.

You may have read in the paper as I did a year or so back of a fifteen-year-old girl, a high school sophomore, who was a straight A student and had just received her first B. As a result, she committed suicide and left a note that cryptically and succinctly portrayed this same problem of achievement. The note said, "If I fail in what I do, I fail in what I am." How cruel and demanding, even brutalizing, high standards can be. In this case it was life eliminating. Far too many suicides result from feelings of not having achieved. It is so intense that the person can't accept himself anymore.

A child raised in this kind of home receives love, but it is a conditional kind of love. He feels loved *if*. He feels of worth and value *only if* he measures up, meets expectations. He lives in a home where two features dominate— too high standards and love which is contingent on measuring up. It is the combination of these two factors that is so deadly.

Every child needs an environment where he receives both conditional and unconditional love. He needs attention and love just for who he is, without any successful performance on his part. This kind of love is especially critical in the early years. In fact, at infancy there should be no other kind of love.

I think one of the reasons God made toddlers so cute and cuddly is that at this stage of life they must have this unconditional love. But when children get older, this unconditional love needs to give way in part to some conditional love. Later in life every child needs to learn that other people's approval requires something from him. He can't expect to be of worth and value to others regardless of how he acts. So you see, there is a rather complex and changing mix of conditional and unconditional love that is desirable in every child's life.

This interesting mixture of conditional and unconditional love comes as no news to the Christian. He is well aware of the unconditional love of God in Christ. God, while we were yet sinners (and thus didn't in any way measure up) died for us. That's unconditional love, and once we have realized that, that "all our righteousness is as filthy rags," and that "by grace you have been saved through faith; and this is not your own doing, it is the gift of God—not because of works, lest any man should boast," then we know that there is no way in which we can measure up. Grace is often referred to as "unmerited favor." The idea inherent here is that there is no way in which we can earn this love of God. It is freely and unconditionally given us in Jesus Christ. This is justification and is never earned! But then there is also sanctification, and that's a slightly different story. Here we as Christians believe that our behavior is important and that God is concerned with and approves of our achievement. Not that we can earn His grace, but we do believe heaven has differing rewards for our performance. The "wood, hay, stubble" passage in Corinthians implies this.

And so it should be in our homes just as in the house of God. We need that fine mixture of conditional and unconditional love, beginning with unconditional love. Once you have established a sound base of existence and identity on that bedrock, then conditional approval can play its role. It's not nearly so threatening to try to measure up if we have learned deep down that we are of worth and value.

The child raised in a home with too much conditional love soon hungers so for approval that he becomes prey to depression. Either that or he becomes power-hungry and achievement-mad.

One middle-aged gentleman, Mr. Reifsnyder, while on the backside of a depressed episode, told the story of his background. His depression seemed to be the result of the inhuman work demands he placed on himself for many years. Working morning, noon, and night he had now in middle-life completely exhausted himself and as a result triggered a depression. He was the second of three sons. His older brother was the athletic type, excelled in football and basketball, and lettered in four sports. The younger brother was cute and funny. His parents and others constantly laughed at him and enjoyed his antics.

As a child Mr. Reifsnyder found he could get his parents' approval and acceptance by being a conscientious and hard worker. In this way he could compensate somewhat for the attention his brothers were getting. He grew to become an exceedingly responsible and diligent adult, and long after the subtle rivalry between brothers was over, he still secured his own approval of himself through long hard hours of work. But now the fourteen-hour days and the six-day weeks had caught up with him.

48

Low Self-Confidence

If our standards are unrealistically high, then it follows that we will think of ourselves as doing poorly, of being inadequate or incapable. The contrast between those high standards and the awareness of our inability to achieve them eats away and eventually destroys self-confidence, and we succumb to hopelessness. The chronic discrepancy between goals and achievements is depressing.

I remember a highly dedicated and compassionate young man who had left a good job as an engineer and had gone back to school in psychology because of his desire to help youngsters in trouble with the law. He eventually set up and managed a half-way house to re-habilitate the youngsters. Working with criminals or juvenile delinquents is not an activity in which you achieve a very high proportion of glowing successes. You have to be satisfied with a handful of turned-around lives compared to the many who continue in the same paths.

Eventually this young man became depressed with what he felt was his lack of success. Yet by many standards it appeared his results were really quite acceptable, if not exceptional. He was in a vocational area where the ratio of successes is abysmally low, and this is no field for someone with perfectionistic tendencies.

I'm also reminded of the wife of an up and coming young executive who had such low self-confidence that when I gave her an intelligence and abilities test she later told me that she had gone home and cried, convinced she had done miserably. In fact she had literally aced a number of the areas. The test was designed so that the problems went from easy to hard, so hard that very few people could get them all. This awareness that she had not known the answers to some of these very difficult

49

problems made her feel she had done very poorly on the tests. When we set our standards too high, we have to literally do the impossible to feel adequate—and that's cruel.

Fear of Failure

The reverse side of this high-need-for-achievement coin is the cringing fear of failure. We are all afraid of failing, but some are thrown by it much more than others, and some are obsessed with the possibility to such a degree that they don't dare attempt anything. At times this can be ludicrous.

I once worked with a young woman who it seemed needed something out of her home environment to occupy her. She was a high school graduate, but it struck me that she was really exceptionally intelligent. She considered college, and when I gave her an IQ test to assess the wisdom and possibility of that venture, I found she had an IQ in the 140 to 150 range. Her fear of failure, however, had prevented her from beginning college. Here she was with intellectual potential that exceeded most medical school, law school, and grad school students, yet she so feared failure she couldn't get herself to enroll even in continuing education courses at a college.

Perfectionism for some may be an outgrowth of this fear of failure. One may raise his standards so impossibly high that it becomes a means of preventing the failure which one is so threatened by and fearful of.

For some this excessive fear of failure is associated with fear of punishment. As children they may have been frequently and even cruelly punished for not measuring up to certain standards. As a result, they are now fearful of trying at all.

50

A child that is punished often for not measuring up soon learns that he is weak and inadequate. He develops a sense of helplessness and inferiority that may not be realistic. He learns negative attitudes toward himself. "I am no good" becomes almost an automatic response to achievement requirements.

Loss of a Parent?

From the research into the childhood of persons who eventually became depressed, we found that frequently they have lost a parent. One study suggests that as high as forty-one percent of depressed persons had lost a parent through death before the age of fifteen. Research such as this, however, does not take into account the percentage of non-depressed persons who have lost a parent through death in childhood. Research that takes this comparison into account still finds a difference, however. The percentage of depressed individuals who have lost a parent is more than twice that found in the histories of non-depressed individuals. So we see that the experience of loss early in life apparently can sensitize one to depression later in life. This is not to say that it is inevitable, of course. We don't want to forget the large percentage of individuals who have also lost a parent early in life who *never* become depressed. Nevertheless, this is a critical lead into our understanding of the causes of depression.

What happens to the person who loses a parent early in life? How does he become sensitized to depression? The science of psychology doesn't as yet have any final answers to these questions. Part of the answer may relate to the dependency tendencies of the depressed person which we'll discuss in chapter six. A number of researchers suggest that this initial, highly emotional loss

51

early in life makes us oversensitive to loss later in life, so that the threat of loss or actual losses causes us to over-generalize its significance in these later situations. The old feelings of loss well up all over again. The despair at not being able to do anything to change the situation to bring this parent back now in this new loss situation also makes us despair and give up. We unconsciously feel there is nothing we can do to stop the loss or to correct it. (Which though true with the death of a parent, is not necessarily true with the current loss or threat of loss.)

Whether or not loss of a parent through divorce has this same effect of sensitizing a child to depression later in life, we can't say. It would, however, seem to be likely, especially in those divorces where one parent is seldom or never available to the child after the separation occurred. The sense of rejection may well become a paramount concern to such a child. We do know that the incidence of orphanhood is higher in the backgrounds of people who become depressed.

The most dominant theory of the cause of depression historically has been the psychoanalytic or Freudian theory. Freud stressed this loss factor and went to great lengths to try to spell out what happens inside a child who has experienced the physical loss of a parent or simply the withdrawal of love and support by a parent during a crucial stage of early development. He thought that a child losing a mother in some way will develop strong feelings of both anger and despair. Because the child has identified with this lost parent and the parent is no longer there to be a target for this rage and anger, it gets turned inward against his own person. The child ends up feeling lonely and abandoned and feeling that he is not being taken care of.

This theory is a rather complicated one (with a lot more dimensions than we have described). Just how valid it is, is not as yet proven or disproven. It is true that feelings of abandonment and loneliness are common feelings for many depressed persons.

Another theory suggests that a child becomes sensitized to depression later in life when in early childhood years he loses mother's attention because a younger child is born and mother has to pay less attention to the older one. As a result, he feels the loss of mother and tries to cope with this loss by getting her attention through being bad. At least he has gotten her attention again. This theory also suggests that the child develops a need for punishment as a means of getting mother's attention. It is true, especially the agitated depressives, that they almost provoke punishment by their behavior.

Lack of Love

Some findings have suggested that lack of love and affection in early childhood may sensitize one to depression later in life. Some rather dramatic findings have been made with children raised in orphanages who, though well cared for physically and nutritionally, had no cuddling or mothering in that sense, and actually died without any apparent cause. The children first went into a stage of complete indifference and depression. There is also some evidence that children who are physically abused are likely candidates for depression. Again, the child who is chronically rejected by his peers for one reason or another becomes over-sensitized later in life to rejection and thus depression.

Saints? Child Prodigies?

Some have suggested that depression also occurs in persons who were generally regarded as "saints" or "prodigies" during their childhood. They were virtually *always* successful and seemed to suffer almost no setbacks as children. Since this is almost the opposite of what we have been talking about, how can that be? It is easy to see how experiences of failure, of rejection, and loss can sensitize one to depression, but success?

The explanation could be that here are a group of children who have not experienced sufficient adversity in their early lives to have learned to cope with it. As a result they not only do not know what to do with failure and rejection when it comes, but it carries far more weight when it finally happens.

As a psychologist I'm often chided for being part of a permissive profession that thinks children are to be coddled and not experience any punishment or adversity. If you will allow me to get a bit defensive, I'll react to that. I'm not sure where that notion got started, but it doesn't accurately describe what I've learned. Psychologists have always been aware of the need for children to learn how to cope. And to learn to cope with adversity a child needs to stub his toe once in a while.

Many parents try very hard to keep their children from experiencing any trauma, failure, or adversity whatsoever. This is not psychologically desirable, for then the child does not learn through his own experience how to cope with these inevitabilities of life. Though parents may be able to keep him in the greenhouse of non-adversive living for a time, eventually he has to face the real world. He will then not have developed the stamina and skills necessary to handle adversity. He has not built up the immunity or emotional resistance that is essential to a mentally healthy personality. I know it's idealistic and therefore difficult to control, but the best state of affairs for the child is neither too little or too much adversity. Never more than what he can cope with, but enough to push his stress tolerance level higher and higher.

Learned Helplessness

A recent scientific advance in the study of depression as "learned helplessness" has gained wide acceptance. This theory suggests that it is not trauma itself that interferes with adapting to life, but *not having control over trauma*. The individual believes he is helpless to control his situation and as a result he doesn't try anymore. He just gives up and this gives in to depression.

In losing a loved one a child must experience helplessness. There is nothing he can do to bring this person back. Many failures in work or school may also have this quality of helplessness to it. If, for example, we can't read very well, we will be helpless to prevent failure in school. Growing old and losing our physical capacities can also precipitate this sense of helplessness.

It follows from what we've learned that parents must be careful not to do too much for a child or protect the child from all suffering. Each child must learn that he is not helpless, that he can master tasks, that he can cope with negative events, that he can fight adversity.

Ambivalence

Ambivalence is another factor in childhood that has something to do with depression. By this we mean that we can have both positive and negative feelings toward another person. We may at one and the same time both like and dislike, even love and hate something or someone. Most of us feel this way, for example, about our government. We like some things about our government and our leaders and dislike some other things.

This concept is critical in understanding human or interpersonal relationships. Whenever two persons get close to each other they will learn more things to dislike about each other as well as things to like. The more intimacy the more ambivalence. In a sense we humans are like porcupines, the closer we get to one another the more it hurts. Mature persons know this and therefore don't expect either another person or a relationship to be either totally good or totally bad. They know that the closer they get the more mixed the bag will be.

But apparently some depressed persons haven't learned this in childhood. They tend to see people in black or white terms. They're unable to view people as complex and multifaceted. As a result they alternate between like and dislike of another person rather than entertain both feelings at the same time.

We have all seen people like this. They become bosom buddies with someone and at that time that other person is all good. But sooner or later—it is inevitable, as they get closer, some things they dislike will emerge. Then their feelings reverse. That person with whom they had become so intimate now receives their dislike, even disdain. I have seen people repeat this process with one person after another—close, intense friendship followed by alienation, withdrawal, and separation. Then they have a new intense relationship that goes through the same sequence.

We suspect that this ambivalence in close relationships stems from difficulties in early life in integrating both positive and negative feelings for one's parents. Parents, being what they are, human and sinners like the rest of us, periodically, if not frequently, botch this job of child rearing and cause dislike on the part of the child. It is, of course, not even necessary to botch it for this to happen. If the parent sets limits as he should, and must if he is to raise the child properly, it is inevitable that the child will dislike to some degree this restricting and limiting figure. So every child should come to have feelings of like and dislike, love and hate for his own mother and father. The outcome should be a unified picture of mom and dad that has both positive and negative parts to it. Hopefully then the child can accept this mix of good and bad.

Some people, however, for some reasons have not been able to integrate these two opposite feelings toward their parents. As a result they go through life expecting relationships not to be characterized by ambivalence, and this is a futile quest.

Children need to learn that these mixed feelings they have for their parents are perfectly okay. I will never forget my little girl at about three and a half years crawling up in my lap shortly after having been disciplined by me for something. She said to me, "Daddy, I like you some and I don't like you some. Is that all right?" What can you say? I don't remember how I responded, but I know that the right answer to that is "yes, that's perfectly all right." For a child to both like and dislike his parent is not only "all right," but quite realistic. That awareness is important for all children to learn.

Unfortunately, some parents rebuke their children for expressions of ambivalence toward themselves or toward their siblings. They insist that children never say they dislike their brothers or sisters or mother or father. To do so is not only poor psychology, but also poor theology, for they have failed to see that as sinners, if nothing else, there is something in them to dislike.

You Can't Blame Your Parents

Before we leave this business of childhood factors that contribute to depression, let's make one thing clear. No matter what happened to you in early life, no matter how your parents may have contributed to or sensitized you to depression later in life, it will do no good to place blame on them. What matters most is not what happens to us, but *our reaction* to what happens to us. Therefore, in the final analysis responsibility remains with us as to what effects bad experiences may have on us.

Besides, as Christians, with our belief that every one is a sinner, we know there are no perfect parents. As a result, absolutely everyone has some bad programming, all of us have some hang-ups as a result of parental mistakes. And where did our parents get some of their hang-ups? Why, of course, from *their* parents, and their parents before them all the way back to Adam and Eve, the real culprits.

It may not be theologically profound but I think this infinite regress of bad behavior relates somehow to the Christian doctrine of "original sin." It is *impossible* (because we are not perfect) to bring up children without, in complex and subtle ways, contributing to personality problems for them.

If we continually blame our parents for our personality or emotional problems, we will lose the sense of being captains of our own behavior and that's dangerous. If we do that we soon start saying things like "I am the poor thing I am because I was treated thus and so by my parents." Even if true that sort of thinking will be very damaging. It will, in fact, set you up for resentment, and resentment is one of the most destructive human emotions. As a psychotherapist and marriage counselor, I firmly believe that resentment is more destructive of relationships (especially family relationships) and persons than any other single thing! Don't cherish resentment; it will destroy you.

"Forgive us our debts *as* we forgive our debtors" is a

healthy perspective here. And as parents ourselves, knowing that somehow we too will contribute in subtle ways to some of our children's problems, we can better forgive our own parents. Every man as a sinner is locked into the prison of time and history. Only God can free us from that.

CHAPTER IV

THE ROLE OF ANGER IN DEPRESSION

THE OLDEST AND HISTORICALLY the most common explanation of depression has been Sigmund Freud's notion that depression is anger turned inward against the self. How this anger gets turned against the self has been the subject of discussion and speculation for forty to fifty years. We won't attempt to spell out all the details of those discussions, but we will try to give you the basic idea.

Freud related the idea that anger gets turned inward against the self to the loss of parent idea we talked about in chapter three. When parents withdraw love and support in early childhood, the child will experience anger as well as despair at this loss. But we can't feel anger at a lost parent, or we would feel very guilty; therefore, we punish ourselves for these angry feelings. Thus anger gets inverted against ourselves.

Self Punishment

The idea we want to get out of all this is that maybe, just maybe, depression is a form of emotional self-punishment. The Freudian view of why electric shock treatments (technically called electroconvulsive shock) can be effective relates to this self punishment notion.

60

Shock treatments serve as punishment and this substituted for the depressed person's need to punish himself and the depression lifts. (We will discuss electric shock in more detail in chapter eleven.)

Anger at Parents

There is also a simpler explanation as to why anger may come to be turned inward. In response to the inevitable restrictions that parents must impose on them ("Don't run in the street," "Don't touch; that pan is hot," etc.) children become angry at the parent, but because they also love the parent, they are afraid to express their anger. They learn to feel guilty and develop a need for punishment for having angry or hostile feelings toward their parents.

In many homes parents will not tolerate *any* angry expressions from their children against themselves. If you will look closely at these homes you will see that there is a double standard operating. The parents allow themselves to be angry and to express it to their children, but the children are simply not given the same right of expression to the parents. I know that as a parent, I'm guilty of this. I can get mad at one of my children for failure to do some chore or something and let them know about my feelings in no uncertain terms. But it comes hard for me to give them the same right of expression when they are angry about something.

There is a most interesting scriptural injunction that may apply here. It is the passage "Fathers, provoke not your children to anger, lest they be discouraged" (Col. 3:21). Here we have an acknowledgement or indication of this relationship between anger and depression or discouragement. Parents need to be careful how they handle children so that they do not provoke anger in them and then turn around and prevent its expression.

The outcome of all these ideas is really the same. Some people just can't express and handle feelings of anger and hostility, and as a result they either pretend the feelings don't exist (denial) and "sweep them under the rug" (repression or suppression) or turn the feelings inward against themselves (intropunitive hostility).

So many depressed people appear passive that it may be difficult to see that anger can be a part of their depression. The example of suicide may help us here. We consider murder a very angry and aggressive act. Well, suicide is also the taking of a life, one's own. It is an aggressive act against the self. And as you probably know, depressed persons constitute the majority of suicides.

Provoke Not

Lorraine had lots of reasons to be depressed. Look at her background. She had been sexually abused by her father when she was thirteen. That happened a number of times until around sixteen she realized and understood what this was all about. She then refused to cooperate. An uncle also had tried to get her to have sex with him when she was a young teenager.

Mother? Well, Lorraine couldn't please her. She was both demanding and critical. She constantly told Lorraine that she was "no good," and "worthless," and demanded that Lorraine do this and Lorraine do that. A slap in the face was Mother's stock in trade. Hardly a day passed without that reminder that Mother was both in charge and did not approve.

Any expressions of anger or hatred by Lorraine were quickly and brutally quashed. Late in her teen years, Lorraine escaped from Mother by a quickie marriage to another youngster from a similar background. Together they nursed each other's wounds. But that didn't last long, as their maturity levels couldn't cope with the demands of married life and a new baby.

Because of this inadequate marriage, its eventual turmoil and the poverty experienced, Lorraine found herself involved with the Salvation Army. She became a Christian through her contact with them. Now she was middle-aged, had remarried a rather passive, somewhat stodgy, but stable husband. They had remained married now for thirteen years, and Lorraine was depressed. Actually she had struggled with depression most of her life, so that was nothing new, but now she wanted to do something about it.

When she talked about herself and her background, she just had to say that not only did she hate her mother, but she found herself frequently wishing for her death. That was hard for Lorraine to admit since that admission triggered volumes of guilt. And as she said, "A Christian shouldn't think those thoughts." She had been asked several times to teach Sunday school but had refused because the guilt she felt for this hatred made her feel unworthy.

It appeared that all the anger developed in childhood and youth had been turned inward. She had learned as a child that other outlets for it would only result in severe, even brutal punishment. She became a very passive, lethargic person. Even now when her husband or child would anger her in some way she would find it difficult to express her negative feelings. She would just mope, get fatigued, and not say much of anything. Often she would go to bed. We had two tasks to accomplish with Lorraine, one to deal with the resentments of the past, and two, to teach her how to assert herself so as to deliver herself (in appropriate ways) of her angry feelings.

Anger as Sin?

Anger is a problem to many Christians. They have learned that expressions of anger are wrong and sinful. As children whenever they became angry their parents either shut off the anger or made them feel guilty and sinful for being angry. They may have even been told that God didn't like the way they were acting or that they needed to confess to God that they were angry.

To consider anger a sin is a horrible and damaging misunderstanding if not perversion of Christianity. The Bible tells us to "be angry and sin not." It also tells us, "Let not the sun go down upon your wrath." We also learn from the Bible of the wrath and anger of God, as well as of expressions of anger by Christ, Himself.

Anger itself is not wrong. Rather, it is how it is handled where good and evil come into play. Certainly we can sin in anger. But we can also deal with and express this anger in other than sinful ways. Christ did. God does. "Be angry and sin not" implies that there are both good and evil, constructive and destructive ways to respond to anger. And "let not the sun go down upon your wrath" implies that we should deal with anger at the time and not let it carry over into another day in the form of resentment or a grudge or hostility. Resentment, you see, is the accumulation of unexpressed anger. And, resentment, I am convinced, is the most destructive emotion in human relationships and in personal well-being.

We can't deal comprehensively with anger here. To do that would involve us in another whole book. But we do need to look at how anger and depression are related.

The danger of course is that if we learn to think of anger as wrong, then we must eradicate aggressive, angry, and hostile impulses and feelings. This eradication can occur in a number of ways. For one thing we can

64

simply deny that we have such feelings. We pretend. Of course, this can't succeed. Anger is a form of energy and this energy must have an outlet. We can't eliminate it; it must be transformed or converted to something else.

Psychosomatic Expressions of Anger

For many people this will take the form of psychosomatic disorders—migraine headaches, asthma, rheumatoid arthritis, gastritis, chronic headaches, skin disorders, ulcers, colitis, lower back pain—you name it, there are many more. I have found so many Christians struggling with one psychosomatic disorder after another that I have speculated that psychosomatic tendencies are a "Christian disease." I would really like to know whether this is true. I have a feeling there may be a higher degree or proportion of psychosomatic involvement with Christians than with non-Christians.

I once worked with a recently retired pastor who had a *thirteen-year* chronic headache. He had tried everything. He had had numerous neurological workups, always with negative findings. He had even been to Mayo Clinic once for a neurological workup. Yet the headache persisted. He tried hypnosis, but to no avail, even acupuncture, but that too provided no relief. He had participated in healing services and had taken pills, pills, and more pills. His wife told me that he had been taking so many pills over the years for his headaches that it had actually become a significant item in the budget.

There was nothing about this man to suggest anger. He actually seemed quite serene given the tension and pressure that a chronic headache would produce. He appeared easy-going and denied having any psychological or emotional problems—almost a little too quickly, I thought.

We explored his psychological history together, and then it started to emerge, just the tip of the iceberg. Yes, he did have some bad feelings about one pastorate he'd been in some twenty years before. He had been unfairly handled by the deacons and elders, especially by a Mr. Larsen who wanted to run the church, the pastor, and everything else. There were serious differences, almost a church split, and lots of unfounded accusations. He was asked to leave. Mr. Larsen led the opposition and was even able to hold up the pastor's salary for a time. On and on the story went, and as it did the anger became more and more visible. But no, he wasn't angry at this unfortunate experience or at Mr. Larsen. He had forgiven him. Just a bad memory now—except he couldn't quit talking about it to either his wife or now to me. The anger that the topic provoked was really quite current.

Then there was that episode with his brother. His brother had encouraged him to put some money into this turkey farm, a "sure thing," his brother had assured him. But that had gone bad, and his brother owed him to this day. As a result they hadn't spoken for years. But he too had been forgiven, I was told.

And his marriage, all forty-two years of it? Oh, no problems there, a "perfect marriage," and he "had seen a lot of them." "The Lord had blessed their home, yes," and he was still very much in love, even if she wasn't responsive or cooperative sexually. She never had been. He had been able to overlook that; "of course he'd suffered deprivation as a result." She'd never want sexual relations and he did; of course he never forced her, though at times he had felt like it. And she was kind of a cold fish; of course her parents were like that, too. And she wasn't the best housekeeper; he'd picked up around the house many times when he knew parishioners would be coming. Keeping the house as well as the church work

66

had been rough all these years.

Then there was this church they were now attending. Do you suppose they had asked him so much as once to take a Sunday sermon? Why, not even a Sunday evening service, mind you. He had been teaching a Bible class, but there'd been a replacement recently. So he just didn't go to Bible class anymore or Sunday evening either if that's the way they were going to be.

Deep, buried resentments. No, he wasn't angry at any of this, but the deep resentments oozed out all over the place betraying his many ready denials. And the longer he talked, the more apparent the anger and resentments became.

Passivity

When anger is viewed as sinful, then passivity becomes the desired norm. A kind of meek, milquetoast personality is likely to be viewed as the Christian norm, the Christ-like personality. But is that what Christ was like? All my life I've heard of the meek and mild Jesus. But where in Scripture do we find that? Certainly He was a sensitive, humble person, but not exactly meek or mild. He was instead a pretty gutsy person who let the Pharisees know in no uncertain terms what He felt about them. Meek and passive people don't refer to others as "white-washed sepulchres."

The danger here is that we hold up a non-assertive, non-angry, meek, and passive personality as the desired Christian. As one of the early church divines once said, "Anger is one of the sinews of the soul." This personality type lacks that quality because he has eradicated through repression, suppression, and denial all awareness and/or expressions of anger.

One research finding suggests that persons that are

67

passive, inhibited, with low self-esteem tend to score higher on hostility measures than do persons not so passive and inhibited. Perhaps if we don't express anger, it becomes bottled up not only in psychosomatic disorders but also in a generally hostile disposition.

It is quite obvious that resentment is both unhealthy and sinful. It is not so obvious with psychosomatic disorders. Perhaps we need to view the channeling of anger into our bodies that can result in psychosomatic problems as sin. If we believe that our bodies are the temple of the Holy Ghost, it is just as wrong to damage that body in this way as in the more obvious forms of abuse through external agents.

Identify and Express It

Just one note of caution here. To say that anger needs expression in no way justifies destructive forms of its expression. Whenever our anger results in hurting either ourselves or others it is destructive. The problem is that most of us fail to distinguish between having a feeling, expressing a feeling, or acting on a feeling. When it comes to anger it is absolutely critical that, number one, you don't deny the feeling when it comes. Identify it—*I am angry.* Have you ever found yourself as I have in the ludicrous position of insisting in highly volatile, explosive and angry terms, "I'm not angry"? How ridiculous! Anger unfortunately (and because, I believe, we tend to think of it as sinful) is more quickly identified as anger by those around us then it is by us.

Once we have identified our anger, the next step is to express it. *How* we do that is critical. Even expressing it is not the same as acting on it. Frequently when doing therapy with angry young adolescents I caution them that even though I will tolerate verbal expressions of their anger (I want to hear about it), they don't have freedom to act it out in my office.

Angry at God?

Maybe we can even express our anger to God. Why not? The psalmist frequently does. I'm amazed at how often the authors of Scripture have the freedom to express their ambivalence to God. You can't, for example, have a severely mentally retarded child without being angry at a God who allows such evil to exist. Of course we need to work that through, but we will never work it through by pretending the feeling is not there. We must identify and express it to God Himself. He can handle it.

Getting the Anger Out

We've found that depression will frequently lift when we give vent to hostility or anger. Dealing with it openly results in reduction of the intensity of the anger and the depression.

I once had a client who was severely depressed. She stayed in bed most of the day even though she had small children. She couldn't get her daily chores done. She was so completely indecisive she called her husband at work many times during the day to have him make simple decisions for her. She had been suicidal. I wanted a psychiatic consultation and possibly medication to cut into the present depth of despair if possible. I gave her three or four names to choose from. She instead went to one close to her home and became infuriated with him, so infuriated that her depression lifted for almost a week! She was so angry at this psychiatrist she couldn't talk of much else. After that anger passed, she slipped back into depression.

Depression as an Expression of Anger Against Others

Some depressed clients I've noticed not only turn anger inward but also make life quite miserable for those around them. I find this more with the angry and hypochondriacal depressive and maybe not at all with the empty depressive. Certainly this does not characterize all depressed persons.

For these people it almost seems that they wallow in depression as a means of hurting others, as if the depression itself becomes an indirect expression of hostility. It's almost as if they were saying, "I'm depressed and there's nothing you can do about it, but it's all your fault, and if you don't give me attention and sympathy, I may get even more depressed or do something desperate." It's a kind of psychological blackmail.

Suicide attempts not infrequently have this characteristic. There's a kind of "see what you made me do" or "now you'll miss me" quality to the notes or communications surrounding the tragedy. They blame others for their bad feelings.

The effect of the depression on those with whom the depressive lives can have a punitive and vengeance quality to it. Take this example. Elaine, a very attractive girl in her late twenties, the mother of two pre-schoolers, had been seriously depressed for a couple months. She had over the period of three months incessantly called her husband at work and at times demanded that he come home immediately or she would "do something" to herself or the kids. The threats were always vague, but she implied suicide. When the husband came home she would force him into a long discussion of whether or not he really cared for her and the children. Or, she would go to bed and leave him to attend to the children. She would say that she was exhausted and just couldn't go on.

70

Before long the husband's job was in jeopardy, and he didn't know how to respond. If he didn't come home, he feared what she might do in her depressed state, but if he did, it hurt his work situation. It was a dilemma. He felt angry and trapped.

After a number of sessions with this client an interesting story emerged. Some time prior to this depression the husband had confessed to this beautiful wife an "affair" he had gotten involved in. He had gotten out of that involvement and felt remorseful about it all. His wife had herself been a beauty queen in a number of local contests as a late teenager and young adult. She had been a sexy and attractive girl in high school and had received a lot of male attention. Even in marriage she had played the role of queen, expecting her husband to pay undue attention to her. That of course wasn't a healthy basis for a relationship, and the husband wearied of his role of worshipful subject and gift-bearing devotee. Unfortunately he took the route of sexual involvement with another party to express his dissatisfaction. This of course was the absolutely lowest blow possible to this wife. How could he have done this, of all things, to her; she who thought of herself as the epitome of sexiness and beauty? Her anger it appears culminated in severe depression in which she made use of every opportunity to make it difficult for her husband. He, feeling guilty and responsible, took as much of these angry, demanding acts as he could until finally his job itself was at stake. Then he insisted that they get some outside help.

At one point during therapy, this husband bought his wife a beautiful long dress for a Christmas present. The dress was much too expensive for their already threatened budget, but if it would cheer her up in some way (and relieve some of his guilt too, I suppose), he felt it was worth it. The first day back at work after he gave the

71

gift his wife took a scissors to it, cutting it into a thousand shreds. Her depression allowed her to get back at her husband, at the same time making it impossible for him to do anything but take it if he wished the relationship to continue. Vengeance and punitiveness were the mainstay of this depression.

Sometimes depressed people are aware that they are making life miserable for others, but they can't seem to control these misery producing behaviors. Take the case of a woman in her early forties. Her husband's job required that they move about 200 miles from the town they lived in. According to him she had not protested this move much at all. She claimed otherwise, however. Once they arrived at the new town she became deeply depressed and suicidal. She insisted they move back to where they had come from. This would force him to seek entirely new employment as his old job was not available. She would call him at work with suicidal threats, and when he came home at night he would have all the housework and cooking to do.

In counseling this woman could see this quite clearly. She said flatly, "I'm rebelling against Jack and this move. I know I'm making his life miserable. He's so good to me, why do I do this?" She couldn't seem to control her obstructive behavior.

Passive-Aggressive Behavior

At times depression and anger seem to result in a give-up-itis. Mrs. Klemers, for example, was so angry at her husband and his treatment of her that she got even by giving up. She was a junior high teacher, so she quit her job, too depressed to teach. Yes, they depended on their combined incomes, but tough, he would just have to find out the hard way what she really had been contributing to this house. She turned over the discipline of the children to him as well. After all, he had incessantly criticized the way she had done it. So now he could try it. The kids too would just have to do without her. They never liked the way she had done things anyway.

Sex had to go, too. At the time they came to me, they both claimed they had not had sex *for over a year.* At first he said this made him furious, but eventually he became apathetic. That in turn made her even more furious. She wanted him to care and be upset with this loss.

She refused to drive the car saying she had a phobia about driving or even riding in a car. He thus had to buy groceries, run errands as well as cook, wash clothes and everything else. She was depressed, couldn't do anything, and there wasn't anything he could do about it, or at least she hoped there wasn't.

In psychology we refer to one category of behavior as "passive-aggressive." By this we mean undercover and indirect expressions of obstructive or uncooperative behavior such as sulkiness, pouting, or prolonged inactivity. Our last four examples have something of this in their depressions. Depression gives them a cover to take out some of their anger and aggressiveness. It thus becomes a double bind for the spouse. You can't walk out on someone who is down and in despair even if you want to escape all that anger or aggression.

Very often this kind of depressed person will be on the "outs" with his doctors or therapist. He will have had a long procession of physicians and/or therapists and expressed this passive-aggressive behavior. To put it simply he has been uncooperative. Medical doctors frequently become the primary target of hostility when they don't find wrong what the patient insists is wrong. Then the person cuts himself off from the very ones who can help him.

In the very first session, even the first few minutes, one of my clients informed me that a long string of doctors and therapists she had were all insensitive and inept clods who failed to pay adequate attention to her problems, and that very likely I too would be like all the rest, and would fail to help her and eventually reject her. She had alienated everyone, *absolutely everyone* in her life, including her own parents and siblings as well as co-workers and every boss she had ever had. She was utterly and completely promiscuous with her hostility. No one could escape it. Even the mailman, deliberately and with malice aforethought, would keep mail and deliver it a day later than when he had received it. She just knew it.

We say that a dog won't bite the hand that feeds it, but that's exactly what some humans do. We entrench ourselves in a vicious circle. We get angry at the very persons who could give us some positive response and reinforcement. Thus we lose the reinforcement we so desperately need, and we cut ourselves off from the very people who could contribute what we simply cannot furnish for ourselves.

CHAPTER V

INFERIORITY FEELINGS
AND DEPRESSION

FEELINGS OF INFERIORITY are the keynote of depression. Those feelings are always there it seems, with very few, if any, exceptions. Neurotics of all kinds struggle to some degree with inferiority feelings, but the disorder where it is most obvious is depression. It will likely be the very first thing you will notice about a depressed person.

Pam was like that. The first thing teachers and students noticed about her was her lack of confidence and her inferiority feelings. She would sit down in a professor's office soon after she had begun a new course and enumerate for him all the reasons why she would not do well in the course. She would put herself down rather cruelly as well as point out all the unfortunate things happening in her life at this time. You couldn't help but feel sorry for her. And it was quite understandable that she feared the course would give her problems and lack of self-confidence. She would suggest that perhaps she should drop the course, but the professor would quickly reassure her that was unnecessary and that he would be happy to work with her in any way that he could and that these personal problems would be "taken into account." She shouldn't worry. When Pam left the professor's office he might check to see how she had done on a preliminary quiz and find she had a high B. From the discussion that had just taken place, he had thought she had probably failed.

Students, too, picked up on Pam's sad demeanor and feelings of inferiority. She often sat alone in the cafeteria looking forlorn. A number of coeds made it a point to sit with her. The talk would eventually come around to Pam's personal problems, problems at home for the most part, and her ever present feelings of inferiority. Pam quickly attached herself to Betty who was confident, had lots of friends, and talked a lot. Betty was also a devout and vibrant Christian who wanted to help Pam. Pam's feelings about herself, her constant berating of herself, really got to Betty, so she set about to reassure Pam of her worth, her value, and her abilities. Betty wasn't the only one. A number of girls in the dorm noticed Pam's hurt and feelings of inferiority and set about to try to make Pam feel better about herself.

Mr. Seamons had the same problem. He was organist at the church and a good one. But every year when it came time to appoint the organist for the next year, he would indicate he wished to resign, stating that it was important that the church secure a truly competent organist who could handle the job the way it should be done. Only after much coaxing and reassurance that his performance was more than adequate would he agree to the position for another year. He was something of a perfectionist, that was obvious. He practiced even minor musical interludes for hours and hours. Church members thought of him as a very dedicated organist.

Seamons, however, never felt capable of playing for special occasions. He was frequently asked to play for weddings but always responded that they should get a good organist for such an important occasion. He would say how poor he was at this or that kind of music or that he got too nervous at such important events. One young couple had heard Mr. Seamons' disclaimers and so had gotten a college friend to play for their wedding. Mr. Seamons, however, was miffed and would hardly speak to them for months.

The church felt badly about Mr. Seamons' "problem." It was obvious to everyone when he wasn't at the organ. Apparently he had had a blow-up with the church custodian, which was completely out of character for Mr. Seamons. He became enraged and completely lost his cool. He passed out and had to be brought to the emergency room of the hospital because they thought he had a heart attack. From the emergency room they placed him on the psychiatric ward. The word that came back to the church people was that he was very, very depressed.

These stories illustrate a number of facets of depression. You have often heard it said that so and so has an inferiority complex. This complex has a number of components, exemplified by Pam and Mr. Seamons. Let's see if we can pull out some of these component parts and look at them separately.

Need for Approval

One component of the so-called inferiority complex is a high need for approval. The person who feels inferior does not approve of himself. As a result he is always searching for the approval of others to counteract this disapproval of himself.

It's miserable to live with yourself if you don't approve of yourself, but that's just what happens to the person with inferiority feelings. Because he feels he is inferior, that he doesn't measure up, he can't approve of himself. And if you can't approve of yourself, what are you left with?

Superiority

You can put up a big front. You can try to fool others and even yourself that you've got it all together. This, of course, comes across as anything but inferiority. Instead it appears as a superiority complex. These people spend all their time talking to others about their successes (usually past successes) or their great skill in some area (which they are currently not choosing to engage in anymore as they've achieved all they want to in that area). Or they vividly describe past exploits and the acclaim they received from others. You see this a lot with college freshmen. They arrive at this new and unfamiliar environment with a group of peers whose approval they desperately crave but don't yet have. Old sources of approval are gone. Some who suffer from inferiority feelings attempt to cope with this need by boasting and begging or, not so subtly, by referring to their magnificent achievements in high school.

Larry did this. As a freshman he had been sent to me by a physician. He had sought help for a severe headache, and, finding nothing wrong, the doctor suggested that Larry talk with me. The school nurse had seen a lot of Larry. So had the dorm supervisor. Larry had, in fact, made something of a pest of himself with both of these people. I heard that he had alienated all his peers in the dorm. He had talked incessantly of his high intelligence and abilities to anyone who would listen, as well as of his athletic prowess in high school. When he came to me he gave me the same treatment. He also told me how his professors remarked on his performance in their classes. Also that he had received this scholarship for college and was currently being considered as a candidate for a special award. Interestingly enough, almost none of this was anywhere close to being accurate. He

78

was at best a B student, but he insisted to his professors that he was an A student who had done A work, and it was only because of their personal dislike or inadequate assessment that he had not received the A. He was furious with the coach for cutting him from the basketball team. Though he was a "walk-on," he had told the coach he had turned down numerous athletic scholarships to come to this school.

Poor Larry. He had deceived only himself by his campaign of superiority. I have seen Larrys go from place to place, job to job, church to church, even wife to wife without facing themselves. Seldom do these Larrys become emotionally disturbed with depression. However, if they do it happens in one big collapse of overwhelming anguish. They may suffer from other mental disorders, however.

One's Highest Goal—The Approval of Others

Another way to cope with the need for approval is to make it the uppermost thing in our mind. Whatever we do, we ask ourselves, what will others think?

Fear of rejection underlies this high need for approval. The person is so sensitive to rejection that he makes every move with the intent of avoiding the rejection of others. He strains for approval and stands on his head to be loved and approved. This is typical of many depressed persons.

They try so hard to prevent rejection that they end up acting funny or strange, and as a result get the very rejection they fear. It's a vicious circle. People see that this person is trying desperately to gain their approval and to please them. They wonder what's happening and move to avoid such a person. So the depressive gets his fears of rejection reinforced.

I've seen this in myself when I've been over concerned with the approval of others. It is just at those times that I say the dumb thing or am up so tight that I can't speak meaningfully to the issue. As a result I feel I've really botched it, and often I have. I have struggled with that problem. The approval of others has meant too much to me, because of my own lack of self approval, and it has caused me to act in ways that I often feel bad about. I might even act superior when that's hardly what I feel inside.

Not Oneself

The person with a high need for approval may never be himself. He conforms to what he thinks others want and will approve of, and becomes divorced from his real self. Or he feels like a hypocrite for always wearing a mask that does not represent how he really feels. And that's depressing! In our Christian society that can be very subtle. We might adopt a certain behavior because it is highly approved by our Christian friends but our real motivation is to gain their approval. One can even enter the ministry or become a missionary for such reasons. Heaven forbid! But it happens. The ministry often involves being in front of people or doing things for them; it is a vocation to which persons with high needs for approval are easily attracted.

Victimized As a Result

With this need to do almost anything to gain the approval of others, we can end up allowing ourselves to be bossed around or pushed around by others. We can be bullied if we have such needs. And, unfortunately, many people would gladly take advantage of that.

Self-Depreciation

Another component of the inferiority complex is self-reproachment and self-depreciation. This dominates the conversation of the depressed person. He feels a need to spell out for you all his lacks, his bad behavior, his shortcomings, his ineptitudes, his failings, his weaknesses, in short his inferiorities, both real and imagined.

A middle-aged mother, Gale, came in very depressed and went on and on with a listing of her inadequacies. She was not a good mother, she was a lousy cook, she didn't keep the house clean, she had no personality, couldn't relate well to others, couldn't make small talk, was not a good child to her own parents, didn't treat them right, was not a good companion to her children or husband, was doing badly at her job (she was a legal secretary), couldn't type fast enough, had no talents or skills, had never done anything right, etc. Conversation with her husband and later with her parents gave me a different picture. Jack, her husband, really had no complaints. She was a good cook, a good mother, he enjoyed her company, had no complaints with how she kept the house—except perhaps she was a bit too fussy. Her parents? Well, they couldn't ask for a finer daughter. The other children had not paid nearly as much attention to them as she had and they appreciated her. They knew she would be there when and if they needed her.

What was happening here? Why this massive depreciation of self when those around her were not only satisfied but unexpectedly pleased with her performance?

Perfectionism

One reason was her perfectionism. This competent homemaker was an unbelievable perfectionist. Though

81

she more than met the expectations of those around her, she didn't come close to the standards she had for herself. In spite of the fact that she now worked full time, she still held herself to the same standards of homemaking that she met when she was not working. She also felt inadequate because she found it necessary to have her husband do some household tasks like carrying out the garbage or picking up groceries. He didn't mind, but she felt as though she failed him. When she got home from work she would feel too tired to make a big dinner and this made her feel worse. Every other year she had completed her Christmas shopping *before Thanksgiving,* but this year she had run around doing it the last minute. (It was hard not to laugh when I thought of how frantic and belated some of my own last minute Christmas shopping has been.) But it was no laughing matter for Gale.

Because she felt short of her own impossible standards of performance, she felt totally inept, inadequate, and incompetent. It's easy to wonder off the top of our heads why this should be so. But take a second look. Haven't you done that, too? I have. I make one bad remark in a speech and I come home feeling the whole address was bad. Or if one speech bombs out, for awhile I may think I have no ability at all for public speaking. I could go on and on with examples of myself, and you probably can too. I see it in counseling every day.

Overgeneralization

For one thing we overgeneralize. We jump from a particular misstep we've made to all of life. We stub our toe and we feel we can't walk correctly. Because we did poorly on one quiz, we feel we just don't have what it takes for college.

The person with inferiority feelings pays attention to

the few bad things he does and overlooks all the decent and good things he has accomplished. He lets some dislike for a particular trait in himself extend to dislike of his entire person.

Apparently King Saul had this problem. Remember how he struggled with depression several times in his life? At one point Samuel said to Saul, "Though you are little in your own eyes, are you not the head of the tribes of Israel?" (1 Sam. 15:17)

We need to see the larger picture, but that's difficult for the depressed person. He typically moves from a rejection of some specific trait or characteristic about himself to a global rejection of his entire personality.

Failure to Maintain Ambivalence

You remember we spoke about *ambivalence?* In every human relationship there will be a mixture of likes and dislikes of other people. The closer we get to any human being, the more things we dislike about them.

Well, we are not only ambivalent about other people, but also about ourselves. I both like and dislike things about myself. I'm a human being, imperfect, a sinner. How could it be otherwise? I don't ever expect to arrive at a point where I will accept totally every aspect of my being, my personality, my body, etc. Not in this life anyway. Oh, as I look back I see progress. I have learned to accept more and more who I am. But the ambivalence is still there and always will be, because as long as I'm in this world I expect to remain quite human, quite imperfect, quite finite. I would rather acknowledge my imperfections than deceive myself that they are not there. I like Roger Barrett, you see, even though some things about him stick in my craw.

The depressed person, however, finds it difficult to be

ambivalent toward himself. If he finds something about himself or does something that he does not like, he gets all wacked out. Then he hates himself. He generalizes that he is *all* bad. He is *no* good. He is a bad parent. He is a good-for-nothing employee. And all of life is bad! I'm no good because I'm unattractive. I'm bad because I lust. I'm worthless because I'm not athletically inclined. I'm dumb because I'm not good at math. I'm a social misfit because I get nervous when I speak to strangers. I'm not liked by other people because Suzy doesn't like me. I'm not a good accountant because I'm not a senior partner. I'm ugly because I have a large nose.

Many psychologists believe this globalization process often gets started in childhood. Parents themselves may have done this to the child. They call the child "stupid," because he failed to shut the door or left his bike in the rain. Or they tell him he is a "bad boy" because he did one bad thing. Or they tell him "can't you do anything right?" when he fails to do a specific chore correctly. Because parents have bombarded the child with global negative generalizations, the child learns (by example) to do this same thing to himself and others. He does not learn to be ambivalent toward himself or toward others. Everybody, including himself, is either good or bad at any point in time. He fails to see that his personality is a mixed bag.

To overgeneralize like this, to say you are worthless because some aspect of your person is deficient is the same as saying that if you have a bad arm the whole body is no good, or if your backhand in tennis is deficient, your whole game is lousy.

The depressed person also tends to make some specific deficit in himself the explanation for all adversity that occurs. He appraises everything negative that happens in terms of this deficiency. If Sharon is too busy to talk to me on the phone, it's because she doesn't want to relate to me anymore because I'm too quiet. So-and-so didn't speak to me at church on Sunday because I'm not good enough for them. That couple didn't return our dinner invitation because I'm not fun to be with. My husband comes home late or goes to work on Saturday morning, therefore, he is trying to avoid me.

Any of these events have a number of possible explanations, but the depressed person reaches immediately for some deficit in himself to explain the event. The whole world rotates around his inadequacies, dances to the tune of his problem. Egocentric? Of course. Just because the focus is on a deficit or problem doesn't mean that the self is not the center.

Self-Depreciation—A Con Job

The depressed person may accomplish—consciously or unconsciously—a number of things by depreciating himself. He may be trying to con you to say nice things about him. Have you ever noticed how almost automatic this is? When someone downgrades himself in front of you, you feel some responsibility to countermand that. I've caught myself doing this—evil soul that I am (at times). I've suggested some fault in a speech I gave, thereby coaxing out a compliment for it. Or I've pointed out some minor negative aspect of what someone is complimenting me on so as to get a bigger dose of compliment. How's that for bad behavior?

Many people fall for this con game for the simple reason that self-depreciation seems so honest and sincere. The person who does this, however, may be trying to con himself. By constantly depreciating himself, he eliminates his own need to feel responsible for his behavior. After all, if I have all these deficits who can expect me to achieve or perform well? He attempts to convince not only others but also himself that he should not be held responsible. He's too weak, too inept, too quiet, not aggressive enough, not wealthy enough, not smart enough—whatever. He hopes to convince himself that he should not be held responsible.

Self-depreciation also acts as a preventative for failure. If we don't evaluate ourselves highly, then we don't have to suffer decreases in self-esteem. If we operate at a chronically low level of self-esteem, then we can avoid sudden reductions in esteem because of some instance of poor performance. Or, if we go around convinced that other people don't like us, it won't come so hard when someone actually does express dislike.

For this reason many depressed persons resist any attempts to buck them up or make them feel better. They fear that if they let themselves think or feel good about themselves, they will suffer sudden or larger drops in self-esteem than if they keep it low. When a person fears that he can't reach some goal or master some task, he then sets about to downgrade the asset required to accomplish that task. It then provides him with an explanation and excuse for not doing it. It also, unfortunately, jams up any or all motivation necessary to accomplish that task or goal.

Fear of Failure

Another component of inferiority feelings is the fear of failure. We have already considered this problem to some degree in chapter three when we discussed the high need for achievement.

Fear of failure makes us indecisive. If we're dominated by this fear we can't make and stick with decisions. We wonder, "suppose that decision were incorrect or there were a better one than the decision I have made." So we vascillate or hope someone else will decide. Or we just stay in the middle until circumstances or others push us one way or the other.

I am sure you have noticed how the depressed person just can't get himself to make decisions, to take initiative, or to arrive at conclusions. Fear of failure is so heavy he does nothing at all. He just sits, sleeps, or withdraws, and avoids situations which require decisiveness or action.

This evolves into a vicious circle. Because he fears failure so acutely, he focuses on success or on pleasing others to such a degree that he fails to pay attention to the task itself. As a result he does a poor job. He may behave stupidly or inappropriately and not use the resources he does have.

He also loses ambition and motivation. "Wouldn't it be awful," he says to himself, "if I remained ambitious in a given area and then didn't make it?" So, he instead reduces his ambition and desire for that particular thing. Then, of course, he feels bad about not achieving, and also for not even trying. He adds guilt to his indecisiveness and lack of motivation. And now he almost has reason to berate and depreciate himself.

Self-Pity and Other-Depreciation?

Self-pity is another part of the inferiority complex. We'll discuss this more in the next chapter when we deal with dependency, but for the moment, let's suggest that unlike self-depreciation, self-pity often becomes *other-depreciation*. "I am the miserable creature that I am because of so-and-so" (parents, often, or spouses).

A young woman told me one time "I'm sullen; I whine; I feel inadequate. And it's all my father's fault." She indicated that over the years had he not treated her in a certain way, she would not now be this kind of a person.

87

I'll never forget an older client, a nurse, whose entire existence had become a matter of self-pity and other-depreciation. Underneath she had devastating feelings of inferiority. She would literally bombard me with complaints about others, how they had mistreated her in the past and how they were mistreating her now. Her parents bore the brunt of the complaints. They had mistreated her. Her brothers and sisters had all received more love and care. She had done all the work around the house, but did they appreciate that? No! Not once could she recall a pat on the back. Yet, if her little sister so much as picked up her own dishes from the table she was rewarded. On and on Mavis went with the stories of her childhood.

Now her parents still demanded a lot of her. They expected her to take care of them in their older years, which, she informed me, she had loyally and faithfully done. Yet she hated them intensely. "Mother still treats me like a child," she would say, then go on to show that it was her mother who was acting like a child. Her parents used her, she would say, because she had never married. "I come home after work and they never talk to me, but they leave me all the work around the house to do." She hated the old home they lived in. She hated the neighborhood. Would she move? Or place her folks in a home? No, that was impossible. She was trapped in this old house with these miserable old people who had never cared for her. She couldn't financially afford any other alternative. And if I thought it was any fun to live with aged people who could do nothing but complain of all their aches and pains day in and day out, I had another guess coming. Nor would they let her have a life of her own. They never had.

And she was livid with rage at her sisters. They ran out on her, she thought, got married, and left her holding the bag at home. She was totally alienated from them. She refused to let them bring their children over to the house as that was just another means of using her. She refused to prepare food and clean up after them just so they could have a good time at her expense. And she had also informed her sisters not to expect any Christmas gifts.

Her hatred was utterly and completely promiscuous. She hated and felt used by absolutely everyone with whom she had ever come in contact. Her colleagues at work were miserable creatures whose sole intent in life was to make her life miserable. "They are semi-human," she told me in reference to her nursing colleagues. She felt they deliberately tried to hurt her by talking incessantly about their children. She told me directly she resented married women. They feel they can take advantage of single women on the job in regard to lunch times and time off, she told me. And they wouldn't talk of anything but their children and their families when she was around. Then they complained about their husbands so much she wondered why they got married in the first place. At Christmastime she took her vacation. "I can't bear to be with those people (the other nurses). I hate to be around people who are happy."

As a young woman Mavis had a tragic automobile accident which had left her with a scar over her forehead and up into her hair. She had tried a number of things to cover up the scar, but she complained that the corrective attempts had only made it worse. She felt she had just been a guinea pig for the doctors, and when the experiment failed, they had just sluffed her off. She had tried unsuccessfully to sue one surgeon. Actually, the scar was not that bad. I had barely noticed it the first time I had seen her, but it dominated her life.

She felt she couldn't go out in public because of this.

The scar repulsed them; she could see it in patient's eyes when she got close to them.

As for the patients in the hospital? They were all a bunch of hypochondriacs who just wanted attention because they weren't getting it at home. Even if they did have problems, they all exaggerated their pain. As for those who had accidents, for the most part it just served them right. The pain was their punishment.

Mavis hated doctors most of all, especially the ones she sought out for her own limitless physical complaints. She felt they would not pay enough attention to her problems because she was a nurse. When they did try, she insisted their diagnosis was incorrect. The doctors she worked with were a bunch of greedy, adulterous lechers who were only interested in stupid, conniving young women who would go to bed with them.

Mavis demanded that I sympathize with her. She wanted pity for all the mistreatment she had suffered in life. If I failed that she would become angry at me, too. No one, absolutely no one, escaped the onslaught of her anger, hatred and rage. She used up so much energy trying to control this massive hostility that she left herself exhausted, depleted, and depressed.

Self-pity, which as you can see is mostly other-depreciation, is exceedingly self-destructive. It easily becomes a habit, an automatic response to *all* trouble. It's similar to alcoholism, yet in many ways worse. Avoid self-pity as you would the plague, even when it's justified. This is not a just and fair world in which we live, and we can't expect fair treatment at all times.

Pride

To say that pride is a part of the inferiority complex appears contradictory, so let me explain. Many people who struggle with inferiority feelings just can't stand to be human or to be sinners like the rest of us. They feel they can't make mistakes and can't live with themselves if they do. They demand that they behave better than others. In fact, the standard they use to measure their own behavior is "doing better than others." That standard, of course, dooms them to inferiority feelings for there will always be someone who can outdo them.

Notice that people who feel inferior often talk about how inferior other people are, it's as though downgrading others causes them to rise by comparison.

They also live in terror of having other people find out about their inferiorities. That's why they won't try. For example, to prevent someone from finding out about a presumed inferiority, they would beat them to the draw, so to speak, by telling them how inferior they are. Therefore, the other party cannot expect them to do well.

Incidentally, many people with inferior feelings develop an excessive need to compensate for their inferiority by some other means. They may try to amass material goods to try to prove to themselves and others that they are not inferior. This having more makes them feel superior as well, and they point it out to everyone. They may compensate by acquiring degrees, or power over others, or clothes, or money. The attention they call to these compensatory things will betray the pride which is at the base of their inferiority feelings.

Secondary Gain

This brings up one of the most basic dimensions of most all forms of neurotic behavior, that is, *secondary gain*. Secondary gain simply means that the person gets something out of the symptoms he complains about. However miserable he may feel or be, this misery produces some

91

dividends for him. The hypochondriac, for example, may get a lot of attention and sympathy (secondary gain) for his many aches and pains. Because he has this leg problem, he gets to sit in this special chair. Because he has stomach problems, he has to have special food.

The neurotic symptoms, whatever they may be, can become an excuse for not achieving or performing at the level this person thinks he should be at to accept himself or be accepted by others. So the symptoms become an escape, a means of saving face. He can evade some difficult task and at the same time have an excuse for the evasion. It is almost as if he is saying, "I could be doing better or I'd be making it were it not for this problem or if I only felt better. If I weren't inferior because of this problem, I could succeed."

These very inferiority feelings lead to a vicious circle of not trying. As a result, the person never succeeds or arrives at the level he expects of himself. Thus he has reason to feel inferior and then depressed.

We might call this a paralysis of the will. This person has no motivation to try. Will power eludes him. Feeling inferior, he fears failure, thus he makes no attempt at all. Feeling hopeless and helpless he gives up before he has even begun. His pride has backfired on him.

Christian Inferiority

When we speak of the need to accept oneself and to feel of worth, value, or even to love oneself, rather than to feel inferior, these concepts raise the hackles of many Christians. They feel that *abasement* of oneself is the Christian norm. Confidence in ourselves, they believe, is, in fact, sin. We're not to have any confidence in self, only in God or Christ.

They cite these Scripture verses to make the case: We

should *deny* ourselves. "If any man would come after me, let him deny himself and take up his cross and follow me" (Matt. 16:24). We should *hate* ourselves. "If any one comes to me and does not hate . . . even his own life, he cannot be my disciple" (Luke 14:26). We should *lose* ourselves. "He who loves his life loses it, and he who hates his life in this world will keep it for eternal life" (John 12:25). We should put others before ourselves. "Outdo one another in showing honor" (Rom. 12:10).

We've learned this in gospel songs such as John Wesley's famous "Beneath the Cross of Jesus":

> And from my smitten heart with tears
> Two wonders I confess.
> The wonders of his glorious love,
> And my own worthlessness.

Worthlessness? Is that the feeling the Christian is to have of himself? (Most songbooks today have changed "worthlessness" to "unworthiness.") Another song tells us we are to be "of sin and self swept clean." And still another asks, "Would he devote that sacred head for such a worm as I?"

We could go on and on with such examples. We have been taught to despise ourselves, to place no confidence in ourselves whatsoever. We have learned that it is Christian to depreciate ourselves and that self-rejection is the way to find acceptance with God. Look at the long history of asceticism in Christianity that seems to say we should abuse ourselves, even hurt ourselves, suffer self-mortification to please God. (A practice, by the way, which is common to many primitive religions.)

The many meanings we have attached to the word love in our culture complicate this problem. We may view love of self as vain and narcissistic self-centeredness, or we

93

may see it as self-acceptance and self-appreciation. We need to differentiate between these two views. Self-acceptance is not the same as self-centeredness.

The Scriptures also tells us that "we are to love our neighbors as ourselves." That implies a high order of respect, caring, and appreciation for ourselves. In the Old Testament we read of the beautiful friendship of David and Jonathan, and we learn that Jonathan loved David "as his own soul." He cared so much for David that the writer compared this to his feelings of affection for himself.

Take the example of the apostle Paul. Paul was a very self-assured and confident man. He even dared to spell out all his accomplishments as an evangel for the faith. He was proud of his accomplishments and told us so. He even had the guts to tell us to emulate him, to follow his example. No Christian door-mat-ism here, no false piety which brushes aside accomplishments as though they were nothing.

Yet Paul had a balanced view. He not only told us of his accomplishments, but he told us of his sinnerhood. He was deeply conscious of his sinful imperfection. So he maintains both realities—a positive self-image together with a consciousness of sinfulness and its capacity for evil in his life.

This larger perspective takes into account all of man, that when it comes to saving ourselves, we can sing the familiar lines, "nothing in my hands, I bring." We can't redeem ourselves for salvation; we must place our confidence totally in Christ. We misapply the doctrine of total depravity when we say there is no good in man. That doctrine simply says that there is not sufficient goodness in man to save himself.

As for being a worm? The idea intended with such symbolism or analogy is not that man is no good or that he is to debase himself, but rather that in comparison to God, man is not much. But that does not mean he is worthless. If we ask the question, "What is man?" as the psalmist did, we find that God is "mindful of him," and has "made him a little lower than the angels," "crowned him with glory and honour" and given him "dominion over the works of thy hands" (which is God's creation). Wow! If God, the great creator of this universe has created me and cares for me as He says he does and has demonstrated that He does by sending Jesus Christ, who am I to despise what God has given His life for?

We read in Romans 12:3 that one is "not to think of himself more highly than he ought to think." Again, the point is not that we are to abuse ourselves or to feel inferior and mortify ourselves. Rather, we are to "think soberly," to be realistic about ourselves. To think more highly than we ought to think is pride. On the other hand, to think less of ourselves than we ought to is wrong as well.

If I am to "in honour preferring one another," then I had better appreciate myself. It takes a very self-assured and confident person to prefer others, to put them ahead of oneself in something. People with inferiority feelings can't do that. They focus so much on their own honor and status (or lack of it) that they are unable to focus on others. When we feel inferior we are self-centered and not other-centered. If you don't believe me, look around you and look within, especially during those moments when you struggle with inferiority feelings.

Finiteness

There is one other dimension I would like to comment on here for the Christian. Not all error is sin. If all error were sin, then the errors of childhood or old age would be reasons to feel badly about oneself. Some of our errors, our ineptitude, our mistakes, our failings are due to our finite condition. God has made us that way. We make mistakes because we are too young to know better, or lack all knowledge so that we are unaware of the consequences of our actions. These are mistakes of our finiteness and not necessarily our sinful condition. We needn't get all inferior and insecure just because we are finite.

Conclusion

I know of no finer note on which to end our discussion of inferiority feeling than that struck in Galatians 6:4. Read it. See what it says to you about inferiority feelings: "Let every man learn to assess properly the value of his work and he can then be rightly proud when he has done something worth doing, without depending on the approval of others."

CHAPTER VI

DEPENDENCY NEEDS
AND DEPRESSION

EXCESSIVE DEPENDENCY NEEDS follow from inferiority feelings for most depressed people. If we feel insecure or inferior then it is natural that we feel we can't rely on ourselves. Instead we depend on someone or something outside of ourselves. If we don't feel we can stand on our own two feet, then we will either seek something to lean on or seek external support or props to hold ourselves up. This is why dependency relationships characterize the lives of depressed people.

Sonja Carlson had struggled most of her life with depression. She had been raised by a very pushy, dominant mother who had never let her learn to stand on her own two feet. Mother had made all the decisions for Sonja—what she was to wear, when she was to speak, her friends, her school activities, what musical instrument she played, when she studied, etc. Mother had even decided Sonja's vocation and schooling. Mother expected her to go into nurses' training, but to her dismay Sonja never became a nurse. After four months of nurses' training, Sonja and Gerald ran away to get married, and Mother had been angry at and hostile to Gerald ever since and utterly disappointed in Sonja.

Sonja was now thirty-seven and the mother of three children. Her marriage to Gerald was not happy, and she could see that she had traded off one dependency relationship for another. Whereas Mother had made all the decisions up to age eighteen, Gerald had made them all since. He was just as dominant as Mother had been, if not more so. He would berate her for not standing on her own two feet just as Mother had done, then turn around and veto any decisions she made. Now, looking back, she could see that it was all there when they'd gotten married. He had been so decisive, knew just what they should do and when. And besides, he could stand up to Mother. That had then seemed so very attractive to Sonja, probably the most attractive thing. She never could have left school and run away by herself. But Gerald worked it all out and made the decision, and now she wondered if she had jumped from the frying pan into the fire.

Sonja had four severe bouts with depression before. Two of them had put her in the hospital. Once she had tried to take her own life. Now she could feel it coming on again, more and more desperate. She had sought out the psychiatrist who had hospitalized her the last time, and he recommended she come to see me and work on some of the marital problems.

With her children in school all day and more free time, she found the house boring. But she had no outside activities and no real friends. Occasionally she went on a wild shopping spree, generally after her anger for Gerald had built to the point she couldn't stand it any longer. Of course, he would be furious with her. It confused him, too, because normally she'd have to consult him about any purchase she made, even little things. These shopping sprees were her way of getting even and expressing anger at him. Seldom would she confront him with her anger directly. Fear kept her from that. But after one of these shopping forays he would scream and holler and make her feel even more inadequate and stupid as he would say. Lately he had even made her return some of the things bought. Then would come the increasingly downward spiral of depression. Not that Sonja was happy in between times. As she herself said it, she could never remember a time in her life when she wasn't depressed, unless it was when she was a small child. Chronic, mild depression broken only by periodic episodes of more severe depression characterized her life.

Fears also dominated her life. She feared not only Gerald and Mother, but she feared thunder and lightning storms, she feared Gerald losing his job, that something terrible would happen to the children, that she'd get cancer, that she was losing her mind, that she wouldn't be able to stay on a diet and lose weight, and on and on and on.

Then she struggled with guilt feelings. Sonja could see that her mother needed her now in old age, but she was still angry with her mother. Sometimes she wished that Mother would die, and those horrible thoughts increased her depression. Mother hadn't changed either. She continued to tell Sonja how to do this and how to do that, along with incessant criticism. Sonja never did anything right, according to Mother. She raised the children wrong, didn't keep the house up, didn't make nutritious meals, didn't know how to do *anything*. A visit from Mother would stretch Sonja out for a couple of weeks at least.

As you can see, Sonja had never been her own person. Her mother kept her from becoming an independent human being, then passed to her husband, who, like Mother, made all the decisions and told her what to do. She hated her mother and often her husband; she hated herself and her inability to get out from under their control enough to be her own boss in anything. Yet she

99

feared making moves toward independence because she was sure she couldn't make it on her own. She was trapped in relationships that angered her and depressed her, but she could not escape.

Reliance on Others

Persons like Sonja show excessive dependency on external sources because they lack the resources inside themselves to stand on their own. Because of their inferiority and insecurity feelings, they neither accept themselves nor have any confidence in themselves. Any approval of their person must come from others. Unlike the healthy, self-assured individual who accepts, approves, and loves himself, the dependent person has to form relationships which supply that for him. So he constantly seeks support, attention, and approval from others. He functions well *only* if he has a *constant* supply of love, support, and reassurance from others, and that, of course, is humanly impossible.

Living Precariously

This makes for a very precarious existence. The dependent person lives in fear that he may lose the people upon whom he relies. Losing them or even the fear of losing them may precipitate depression. It's the same for the person who is overly dependent on financial, professional or social status. The loss or the threat of loss of one of these may precipitate depression.

These dependent people live precariously because when stress increases in their lives they depend on external agents to increase proportionately their support and acceptance. They cannot turn within themselves for increased support. To maintain their self-esteem under stress and threat they must rely on positive feedback and support from others. At the same time they have less control over external agents of support so they live with the fear that that support may not be there when it is needed. When signs of threat or stress come into their lives, they panic and show exaggerated concerns and attachment on whatever or whomever it is they depend on.

Exaggerated Needs for Affection

Dependent persons frequently show an exaggerated need for affection. Because they don't love themselves, they need desperately to have others love them. They become love addicts needing a fix whenever they feel unloved and uncared for. They demand or beg others to love and care for them, and they live in a perpetual state of greediness for affection.

They contract relationships with other people out of need, i.e., their own need for constant assurance, support, and stability, so they often attach themselves to someone dominant, decisive, and controlling. Though such a relationship provides them with the stability and confidence they lack in themselves, it does not provide them with opportunities to develop their own internal sources of self-esteem and independence. Therefore, they remain dependent and subject to depression whenever they can't get their fix from others. That was Sonja's problem.

Seeking Affection at Disastrous Costs

The dependent person may also lay himself open to abuse. Others can easily take advantage of him. He becomes a sucker for attention and approval and may even

101

go out and seek it at the cost of disaster.

One of my clients, Betsy, did that and seriously jeopardized the enduring relationship and support she had. Betsy had little or no self-esteem. Her parents had abused her. She never had felt loved by them. She couldn't please them. Her father was an alcoholic nonentity who cared neither way. She has *no* memories whatever of being hugged or kissed by her parents. She remembers only whippings and slaps across the face. As an adult Betsy married a stable but unexciting man much older than herself. When he ignored her exaggerated demands for affection and approval, she got angry and desperate and formed illicit relationships that gave her the physical and emotional support she felt she couldn't live without. When her husband found out about her affairs, what little support she had in her life was cut off.

Next she became furiously jealous and fearful of rejection by her lovers. If they failed to contact her for awhile, she would impulsively contact them. Inevitably, these relationships ended, resulting in even more rejection for her. On top of that, they left her feeling guilty and depressed. As she told me, "I feel so guilty about all the things I've done, I'm afraid I'll end up in an institution."

I've seen this again and again with severely dependent persons. They resort to means of securing the affection and support they so desperately crave thereby reducing what little self-assurance and respect they do enjoy and jeopardize whatever support they have been able to acquire.

One of the beautiful dimensions of the Christian faith is its offer of acceptance and approval to the unloved such as Betsy. In the love of God through Jesus Christ, they can find approval and acceptance by the creator of the universe Himself. We can't do any better than that. However, the Betsys in our world find that hard to believe until they see it lived before them in the form of a Christian.

Manipulative Con Games

Because the dependent person can't risk possible losses from standing on his own two feet, he invents ways of maneuvering others to do his thinking and deciding for him. He learns to manipulate them toward fulfilling his needs and demands. Because dependent types are convinced they can't meet their own needs, they must get others to satisfy their needs for them.

One ploy they try is playing weak or stupid. They make self-depreciating comments to elicit the other person's interest, sympathy, and help. This happens frequently in psychotherapy. Dependent individuals display in scores of ways reasons why the therapist should take charge of their lives for them. They have a barrage of questions about what action they should take about minute aspects of their lives. They ask the therapist to make decisions for them. After they have spelled out in detail the problems they face, together with vivid descriptions of why they can't meet these problems, they then plop the problems onto the therapist. After all, that's why they've come, that's what they're paying for. They expect the therapist to deliver the goods for them, and thus refuse or avoid working on their problems themselves.

If a therapist falls into this trap, he is doomed to a role of meeting the needs which this person ought to be learning to meet for himself. The therapist may, if he falls for this manipulation, find that he is just one of a long string of persons upon whom this dependent person has tried to place their dependence. The therapist of course can't take total responsibility for the well being of the client, and the result is bitter disappointment.

When Help Becomes Harm

Unfortunately many well-intentioned Christians or do-gooders fall into this trap. I've seen it happen with ministers frequently. The parishioner, often a female in this case, will come and play all the chords of need and self-depreciation in a grand symphony of pity and neglect. Unwittingly, the minister in his well-intentioned but naive desire to help, moves in to support, back up, and even make decisions for this pathetic soul. The results, of course, are self-defeating for both. The relationship sometimes gets extremely complicated. The minister eventually feels angry and put upon and doesn't know how to get out of the relationship without rejecting the person or again making them feel inadequate and incapable. Sometimes the minister finds that he has become a replacement for someone else, and has allowed the dependent person to express anger toward the person he previously depended on. Since a wife may previously have depended on her husband, you can see what complications this brings.

I've seen this happen frequently in the college setting. A dependent person will seek out those who provide the support, guidance, attention, and affection they can't provide for themselves. The helper then becomes ensnared in a relationship that quickly becomes much more complicated and demanding than he had intended. Next, if the helping person pays attention to other people, the helpee becomes envious and increases his self-depreciation. He tries to meet the competition and suck the helper into an exclusive relationship. In fact, he may become a leech, constantly in the other person's dorm room, wanting to eat every meal with him, study with him, etc. Eventually the helper gets fed up with the relationship and ends it rejecting the person he originally wanted to help. Now the person needing help is even more convinced of his worthlessness.

Needs Differ From What He Thinks He Needs

The dependent person really needs to get in touch with his own power. He needs to learn how to get the goodies of life by more appropriate and less destructive means. If he gets what he wants through pity and pleadings, it will lead to only temporary gratification. He ends up as bereft of selfhood as he began.

We may compare him to a car without fuel. You can push a car and it will move, but take away that external source of power and the car stops. In the same way dependent people sit and wait until someone comes along and pushes them. When that person gives up they wait again for the next push. The dependent person needs to get his own fuel, start his own engine, and drive the car himself. Until he learns that, he will always need a push, and there are enough do-gooders around to do it. Eventually, however, they all get weary and give up.

Ellen had always been dependent and manipulative. When she came to me she was in her third marriage with a do-gooder who was ready to give up. She could see that Jerry was near the end of his rope and she was getting very panicky. The more she saw him pulling away, the more she demanded his love. That had gone on between them since their courtship.

At first it seemed rather nice to Jerry to have someone who constantly requested his love. He felt big, important, and needed. Now, however, it was irritating and exasperating. Whenever he went off to work (he worked nights) leaving Ellen alone, she felt abandoned and lost. She would then call him repeatedly at work. He didn't mind that at first, in fact, it proved to him the intensity of their love. Before long she claimed she was desperately sick and he would have to come home immediately. She was *always* getting sick. It seemed she had a hundred illnesses or disabilities of one kind or another that only bothered her when she wanted some attention. She had these awful back pains where she could neither sit nor stand. The *only* thing that would relieve them was a certain kind of massage that Jerry did that would take about two hours before there'd be any relief for her. In their eight short months of marriage, they had made four frantic trips to the emergency room of the hospital, only to be given a shot or tranquilizer and told to consult with her physician the next day. Ellen had seen more doctors in the last three years than you could believe. Most of them she found to be highly inept and uncaring, so had sought out one new one after another.

The calls to her parents really annoyed Jerry. After he had refused to let her call him at work at night, she would make these long distance calls to her folks, and the bill was getting ridiculously high. One time when he had left for work in a huff after a fight, he came home later to find her mother there consoling Ellen. Ellen had called her in a state of panic saying their marriage was over and could she come and just talk to Jerry.

One time Ellen had a problem with her boss at work. He had criticized her, and she felt the criticism was unjustified. Ellen's mother was in the same line of work, so Ellen asked her mother to come and talk to the boss. And Mother actually came. If you can believe that, you have a good idea where Ellen's problem began.

It also troubled Jerry that she constantly "put herself out for other people so she could get praised." When they didn't come across with that praise she was furious with the person, then she'd take it out on Jerry. Her boss generally ignored this and that increased her rage and

106

frustration. On those evenings she talked to Jerry about nothing else.

Recently her boss told her that unless she could figure out how to do some things on the job for herself, he'd have to let her go. Apparently she constantly asked for advice about how to do this or that, or cried on his shoulder for one reason or another. "I have to be praised a lot," Ellen informed me, and this boss was just "not the kind she needed."

As Jerry looked back he could see they had gone from crises to crises in both their courtship and their marriage. He could see she had created the crises so that she could be soothed. And now when he refused to respond that way, the crises got more frequent and more serious. It looked very much as though Ellen was on the brink of destroying her third marriage, and *she was not yet in her thirties.* (My first impulse was to bring Mother in and spank her, but that seemed rather unprofessional.)

Overly Sensitive to Criticism

We can see clearly in Ellen's case one characteristic of the dependent person—over-sensitivity to criticism. Criticism utterly floors and demolishes them, especially when it comes from those on whom they depend. They have so few internal resources and depend so much on external sources, that criticism from without has a higher impact than it normally would. Therefore, they will often try to prevent criticism by beating others to the draw. They criticize themselves before anyone else can. Then, too, outside praise will mean more. Or, they may so ingratiate themselves with others they block any criticism at all.

I have an Irish Setter like that. Setters are, as you know, very sensitive animals. Whenever my dog senses some criticism or punishment about to come her way, she becomes the epitome of ingratiation and puts on a pitiful act. At this point she will do absolutely anything I ask. With her tail between her legs, head down and ears at about half-mast, she looks for all the world like the most forlorn and piteous of creatures. She has a purpose, of course, the same one as the dependent person who so mercilessly criticizes himself. Who can criticize or punish one who already feels so badly?

Secondary Gain

We have referred to secondary gain before, but nowhere does it have more direct application than with dependent people. Secondary gain, as we said, refers to the ills of the neurotic person which may, in spite of distress, provide them with some benefit. At a secondary level (not necessarily conscious), they hope to achieve some goal by having these problems.

The most obvious dividend is attention and sympathy. Nurses tell us this is common with people who are physically ill. We all regress a bit at these times and expect attention and sympathy, and we're easily irked if we don't get it. A client told me of a mother who wrote a nasty letter to her grown daughter that she hadn't seen for over three years. The mother had been sick and the daughter had not come around or made any contact with her. She hadn't expected attention when well, but she did expect it when sick.

Getting attention by being sick or inferior is secondary gain. I've had patients tell me they have daydreams and fantasies of getting attention by being hurt. One gentleman told me he has a recurring fantasy of being hurt on the job where the company nurse attends him. Then he is brought to the hospital where the nurses there attend him. He even had specific people who served in these nursing roles. Another shy young lady told me of recurring fantasies of an auto accident where people *had* to pay attention to her.

One hazard of hospitalizing depressed persons is the secondary gain they secure from it. One woman told me, "it felt good to be in the hospital. Everything was taken care of." She felt protected from the demands of her family and job. "I'm looking for a sanctuary, a refuge," she told me.

Misery Enjoyed

This makes us wonder whether or not depressed people actually enjoy their misery? That is certainly true for some but not for all.

Depression can also relieve one of responsibilities. People just can't expect as much of you then, and they give you the benefit of the doubt. After all, how can they expect you to accomplish thus and so when you are, if nothing else, completely fatigued?

To get help, the dependent person must acknowledge secondary gains. The therapist must also understand them. If he doesn't he may work long and hard but accomplish very little. The person must also face the question, do you really want to get better, or does your misery provide you with benefits you don't want to give up? Jesus asked the cripple at the Pool of Bethesda, "Do you want to be made well?" Wasn't that question unnecessary? Here was the man, obviously crippled and at a place of healing; of course he wanted to be made well. Or did he? Likewise in the therapy room, a place of healing, the question has to be asked carefully in virtually every neurotic disorder. Are you willing to lose the benefits your problems provide for the gains and responsibilities of health? This comes hard for the dependent person because the benefits of independence are often unfamiliar or new to him.

Sympathy

The dependent person craves and seeks out sympathy. We all need love and approval, but sympathy is a form of approval we can do without. It's a form of approval we can get however low our standard of achievement and regardless of our level of performance. It's a kind of approval we get by *not* making it. When sympathy becomes a substitute for genuine approval and love, it destroys. Sympathy won't change the personality factors that put us in need of sympathy in the first place. When you find yourself looking for sympathy be careful, very careful. You may get it when it's the last thing you need. It may, in fact, prevent you from getting what you really need.

Sympathy is emotional welfare. You are on the dole psychologically. If you get too much, it may prevent you from looking for the employment you need. It will also hurt your self-respect if continued. You get sympathy for being needy and poor, but that's not something you want to cultivate. Do you see the vicious circle? Recite your problems only to those who can help. Some dependent persons avoid therapists like lazy people avoid a job. They want contact only with those who will sympathize with them, not with those who will help.

Roots of Dependency

In the cases of both Sonja and Betsy, we saw some clues as to why they had become such dependent creatures. Sonja's mother was controlling, bossy, and pushy. Betsy's parents were mean, vicious, and abusive. Let's look at some other factors that lead to dependency.

The doting mother and father who overprotect the child can set the stage for dependency. In their desire to insure the child no hurt or harm, they clear all obstacles from his path. They make childhood too smooth. As a result, he doesn't learn how to cope with problems. He learns to depend on Mom and Dad to take care of things. When he runs into problems, he automatically goes to his parents and they do for him what he needs to do for himself.

We've all seen this happen often in neighborhood spats or sibling fights. Johnny gets into a tiff with a neighbor child over something and comes home and cries on mother's shoulder. Mother then goes out and intervenes. Johnny fails to learn to resolve his own disagreements with others. Not only has he not learned that, but he has also learned that the way to cope with interpersonal problems is to get mother or father to intervene for him. Later in life his wife may wonder why her husband is always coming to her with complaints about the neighbors, or the people at work, or the relatives and wanting her to do something. Instead of learning to cope with problems himself, Johnny has learned to depend on someone else. Learning to cope is a painful process for children, but there is no substitute for it.

Betsy's background, though quite different than this, can also foster dependency. In this background the child is so punished and abused for trying things, that he simply learns not to try anymore. He has been so mistreated that he fears to put himself forward or to try things, for fear of the consequences. This person will not run to others to bail them out as Johnny might have done. Instead he withdraws, letting other people do what has to be done. People like this automatically attach

111

themselves to someone who will take initiative, who does not fear the consequences of action.

In both cases the dependent person will feel "I can't live without him or her." Then they overreact to situations which threaten the loss of this person. They make extreme, absolute judgments at those times and thus set themselves up for depression even before the loss occurs.

Hating Those Upon Whom One Depends

I find it intriguing that feelings of anger and hatred for the person upon whom one depends get all mixed up with feelings of reliance and need for them. We can have both at the same time. In chapter four we referred to this as ambivalence. This, of course, makes the relationship of the dependent person very complex and confusing, both to themselves and to those upon whom they depend.

I think of Myrna as the epitome of these ambivalent feelings of dependency. She felt inadequate and inept. She didn't dare try anything—establish friendships, develop work skills, get involved in hobbies, develop interests, nothing. She had pretty much rotted away at home for most of the eighteen years of her marriage, and she was very dependent on her husband. He made *all* the decisions. All of them. As a lawyer, that came naturally to him. He kept the books, determined their social life (it revolved entirely about his professional life), chose their friends, planned their vacations, set their budget, even decided how they spent their time.

He didn't mistreat her, at least not deliberately. They had a good home and material goods, but they lived separate lives. He played a lot of golf in the summer and hand ball in the winter. They belonged to the country club, but she never went there except for the social events he insisted they attend. When they went to things like that he did all the talking for them. It wasn't that she didn't say anything, it was just that others had to start the conversation.

In the last year the marriage has seriously deteriorated. Suddenly she refused to cooperate in things he felt were important. She wouldn't go to social events he had arranged, so he went alone. She ran up large charge account bills for clothes, so he closed up the accounts and took away her credit cards. She refused to have sex with him, so he forced her several times. They even had several physical fights in which she had thrown some expensive dishes and a vase. In sheer frustration, he put his fist through a door in the kitchen. When she got wild as he described it, he would just hold her still.

This kind of fighting had been taking place when they came to me. They were having no sexual relations, in fact, they weren't even speaking, and had slept in separate rooms for almost four months. Myrna had filed for divorce on the grounds of mental cruelty. Added to that, she chose a lawyer she knew Vic despised and would be upset with her for engaging.

Myrna insisted Vic leave the house, and when he refused, she refused to prepare meals for him. They were about as far apart as you can get and still live under the same roof. The closer the final hearing came the more Myrna started to panic. She rehearsed in detail all the fears she had about being on her own. She was sure she couldn't make it. Then she rehearsed her anger at Vic. As the hearing approached, Myrna got sick and it had to be postponed. That lessened the panic, but the same thing happened as the new date approached. Although Vic opposed the divorce, he had moved out to gain some peace and sleep. A week before the hearing they had to talk and hopefully agree on some financial settlement

113

matters. They ended up having sexual relations and again the hearing was postponed. Myrna said she was willing to reconsider but would not completely call off the divorce. She wanted to see how he'd continue to act before she finally made up her mind. Also, to get back together he'd have to agree to reinstate her credit accounts. When he refused that, she called her lawyer and tried to reinstate the divorce proceedings. And so it went.

Myrna depended on Vic yet hated the fact at the same time. She despised herself for being so dependent, but held him responsible for it. So she hated him for her dependency on him. She hated the dependency relationship but feared the independence she needed to get out of the marriage. Back and forth, back and forth it went. She couldn't get in and she couldn't get out.

This combination of anger and dependency is common. Often the dependent person will not express his anger directly. That would threaten the relationship so his anger goes underground. He expresses it indirectly in what we call passive-aggressive behavior. That is, he expresses his resentment in passive ways that don't overtly attack the person upon whom he depends.

With Parents

We see this a lot with adolescents. Have you noticed how often mid to late adolescents get depressed and rebel at the same time? They still feel dependent on their parents, but they hate that. They want very much to be independent persons, so they vascillate back and forth. Periodically they go all out in some rebellious act to prove they are independent. They say in effect to their parents, "I don't need you," but they are also trying to prove it to themselves. If they don't dare to be that direct, they might make life difficult for their parents by opposing

114

whatever the parents want them to do. They're angry at their dependency as well as the parents upon whom they are dependent.

Gary felt trapped that way. He still lived at home, but fought constantly with his dad. At twenty he worked in an office and hated it. Though he was a handsome young man, he had no friends. He got together once in a while with some of the other guys in the office, but he felt uncomfortable with their values. He really wanted to go to college, but his father had insisted that college was a total waste of time and money. He needed to get a job in a good company and work his way up, according to his father.

Gary felt completely dominated by his father. No matter what the topic of conversation he felt his dad would always put him down as well as anyone who supported him or made him feel good. His Aunt Julie encouraged him and stood up for him, but his father claimed she babied him. She encouraged him to date but his parents said he shouldn't spend the money. When he bought a car on his own this last year, his dad said it wasn't worth what he had paid for it.

Gary had had a girl friend, one who had ditched him for another boyfriend she said she "was more interested in." That had really gotten to him. And at that point he came to me depressed. He could barely get up and get to work and had called in sick a number of times and stayed in bed. He knew it was just that he was down, but had told his mother he had "stomach problems." On these days he had thought of taking a bottle of pills. Wouldn't his parents feel bad then when they came home from work? But those thoughts scared him. Also, he couldn't get his girl friend off his mind. Not that he liked her that much, she had been so pushy telling him where they were to go and when. Aunt Julie had arranged for him to meet her in the first place and that bothered him. But it bothered him how she had ended it and that she preferred someone else to him. Gary told me he just couldn't get himself to ask out girls, because he knew there were so many other fellows they'd rather be with.

Gary hated going home after work, but he didn't have anywhere else to go. Dad would just put him down for something at dinner, he knew that. The more Gary talked to me about his father, the more apparent his longstanding anger and resentment for him became. At the same time he was very dependent on him. Several times his dad had told him to move out of the house and get a place of his own, but almost in the same breath he would tell Gary that if he did he couldn't make it on his own. But Mother would say later that Dad hadn't meant it, so Gary continued to live at home.

Getting Gary to think of attending college, to change jobs, to form friendships or socialize, or to move out of the house was like pulling teeth. As much as he said he wanted these things, he feared the independence or initiative they required. His feelings of dependency had him trapped.

Misery If You Stay, Misery If You Leave

I have seen many marriages where the dependent party has made life miserable for the more independent one, or where the more independent party snuffs out any independent tendencies or moves by the dependent one. They each make life miserable for the other, and at the same time keep them trapped in that misery. I have seen the dependent one constantly provoke the other, but when the more independent person takes steps to break the relationship, the dependent one threatens suicide or induces guilt feelings in the other for abandoning them after making them like they are. It can get very vicious.

I remember one such case. The wife, in her fifties, complained of everything her husband did. He escaped this in a constant round of bowling leagues. (She hated to bowl.) So she refused to cook meals or clean the house. Even though she didn't work outside the house, she claimed to be too exhausted to clean the house and he had to do it. In spite of all her complaints she still wanted the relationship to continue. She told me, "I'm a weak person and don't want a divorce." He had wanted one for years, but whenever he headed in that direction she either got very ill or threatened suicide. Once she told me, "I'm afraid of happiness because it can be taken away from you." She made happiness an impossibility and thereby never lost it or had it taken from her.

Indecision

Indecisiveness accompanies dependency, that's obvious. It's important to you that others make decisions for you. I saw a young man once, a computer programmer, who had approached a wedding date four times and had backed off each time, the last three times with the same girl. He had dated her for four years, and while he couldn't bring himself to marry her, he also couldn't leave the relationship either. They had broken up numerous times, but whenever he thought of forming any new relationships, it scared him and he'd soon get back with her. Once, they had come up to twenty-four hours before the wedding. The invitations were out, the cake ordered, the church arrangements made, and he cancelled everything. He couldn't move forward to marriage, and he couldn't move back and out of the relationship. He couldn't decide to go either way.

117

Apathy, Lack of Motivation

Many dependent persons seem very apathetic, devoid of any motivation to improve their lot, unable to employ whatever assets they have. They seem to suffer from a paralysis of the will.

I think of two young married women, both very dependent on their husbands. One was very intelligent and very attractive and could pick up any new skill almost instantly. The other was artistic, dressed magnificently and highly competent in interior decorating. However, both were very depressed and depleted with seemingly no ability to exert themselves. They both would endlessly criticize themselves and refuse to acknowledge the fine assets that they had. (However, if anyone criticized them in these asset areas, they would become incensed.)

We learn from these cases that this apathy and seeming lack of motivation may really be quite deceptive. Actually, they had very *strong* motivation and drive to *avoid* constructive activities. They were highly motivated and determined not to be motivated. No matter what encouragement their husbands provided them (and it was substantial in each case), it was all to no avail.

Dependent Females

You may have noticed how often I have referred to females in this study of depression. I am simply reflecting real life. More females struggle with depression than males at about a three to one ratio. The reason for this, I believe, lies right here with this matter of dependency. Females in our society have been taught to be dependent and passive. Depression is just a gross exaggeration of these dependent and passive patterns. Also, females have lacked a basis on which to establish their identity.

Most men find their identity in their vocation. In this role they find prestige, status, and security. Not so for females. Their major source of prestige, status, and identity comes indirectly through their husbands and their husband's vocation. (The doctor's wife is a good example.) Since so much has been written about these problems recently, I will simply allude to them here. But it does, I believe, explain in part why so many more females than males get depressed.

Another reason that may help to explain why more females than males get depressed is that alcoholism is a common refuge (and thus cover-up) for male depressives. Perhaps many of the males who get classified as alcoholics are really cases of depression. Another possible explanation is simply that women in our society may not be as threatened as men and admit to having emotional problems. If they are depressed they admit it and go for help. We've built a stereotype of the male that makes it difficult for men to ask for outside help. This may explain why the suicide rate, ulcer rate, and incident of heart problems is so much higher for males, but emotional problems are higher for females.

CHAPTER VII

GUILT AND DEPRESSION: FALSE GUILT

THE RELATIONSHIP BETWEEN guilt and depression is frequently a chicken and egg kind of problem. It's difficult to tell which has caused the other.

Guilt can occur for many reasons—good and bad. Also, many people who probably should feel guilt, don't, and many who are overwhelmed with guilt often have no good reason to feel that way. Some writers try to simplify the idea of guilt, but it can't be done. Some claim that *all* guilt is a result of sin; others dispose of guilt as an unnecessary artifact of a previously religious society. Both views are overstated.

Before we can come to grips with whether or not guilt is appropriate or inappropriate, relevant, or old-fashioned, we need to look at a number of the reasons for which people feel guilty and eventually depressed.

Misbehavior

Guilt can be the simple, straightforward outcome of misbehavior. If we fail to live up to our values, we should feel the knife-edge of our consciences. If we believe we ought to behave thus and so and we don't, it follows that we should feel guilty. That should be true for anyone who has values, not just for Christians. The Christian, of course, derives his values from Scripture. If he violates these maxims he should feel guilty. Two and two are four. We'll call this kind of guilt "real guilt" and devote an entire chapter to depressions that stem from it.

Guilty For Not Being Perfect

However, we may also feel guilty for not measuring up to standards that are too high, inappropriate or perfectionistic. In the chapter on childhood factors that contribute to depression, I told you that many children have impossible achievement standards laid on them by parents and others. These people often feel enormous guilt for failure to reach the unreachable. Every therapist has seen this kind of guilt with depression. The lady who, motivated by guilt, gets up at five in the morning to clean an already spotless house for fear that it doesn't "measure up." The wealthy doctor who drives himself mercifully because he hasn't achieved and exhausts himself in a guilty depression. Remember Amy, the straight A sophomore in high school who took her own life when she received her first B in a course at school?

Some people feel guilty and blame themselves for family quarrels, or the death of a loved one, or for going on a vacation, or having sexual relations with their spouse, or even driving a car. It may sound odd or extreme, but as I said, every therapist has seen this kind of pathological guilt frequently. We call it "false guilt," false in the sense that it does not violate the person's values or God's values as he sees it. Nevertheless, he feels very guilty.

Guilty For Not Pleasing Others

It is also true that we may feel guilty whenever we think that those whose love we seek do not accept our feelings or behavior. A child, for example, may feel guilty for not pleasing an impossible father or a nagging mother.

Exploitive Guilt

We may use guilt to exploit or manipulate someone or to placate authority figures. In this we don't genuinely feel guilty or regretful at all. One study found that true with a group of manic-depressives. They expressed guilt as a means to an end; it wasn't a sincere feeling of self-reproach.

So we can see that guilt can be many things, some good, some bad. First of all, we will look at some false guilts which Christians often experience. Then, in chapter nine, we will discuss real guilt.

Paul Tournier, the Swiss doctor who has written so many excellent books on the Christian's experience with emotional problems, has focused on this issue of real and false guilt in *Guilt and Grace*. He suggests a simple dichotomy, i.e., that the violation of the laws of God should involve real and appropriate feelings of guilt, but that the violation of the laws and mores of man which may also result in guilt feelings are not necessarily violations of God's laws and therefore may result in unnecessary guilt feelings.

Consciences Differ

I agree that every Christian must come to grips with this if he is to know the voice of God in his life. Virtually every human being has a conscience of some sort, and this conscience has been molded and shaped on the potter's wheel of family and cultural background. It is here, largely in formative years, that one learns what is right and what is wrong. But what one culture or family or church group may consider right or wrong is not the same as what another group thinks.

I live close to a major center of Amish folk. One time I toured that area with some zealously evangelical friends who became increasingly impressed with the disciplines of these Amish folk—no motor-driven vehicles, no electricity on their farms, plain clothing. They seemed so devout, their standards so very high. The Amish, of course, disapprove of these practices and consider them sinful. Later we came across two elderly Amish gentlemen standing on a street corner, puffing away on pipes. In conversation with a storekeeper in the area, we learned that these folks drank alcoholic beverages. Suddenly, the admiration and respect my friends had for the Amish turned sour. Drinking and smoking were crucial taboos in the value system of my friends, so they were now disappointed with these plain people.

Yes, backgrounds differ in determining right and wrong, so consciences differ. Therefore, every Christian must examine his own conscience in the light of God's Word and collective human experience. Paul tells us in Romans not to be conformed or shaped by this world. Unfortunately our conscience is one of the last areas of our personality to undergo the scrutiny of the Holy Spirit. We seldom think of it as having been shaped by "this world." So many of us have been raised to cloak our consciences in religious garb, to think of them as a part of our nature which is already godly.

This of course is pharisaical. Have you ever asked why God sent Christ right into the middle of one of the most religious groups going, the Pharisees? Why didn't He choose some obviously heathen part of the world? Why not to the savages or to a cannibal society?

I suspect that God sent Christ to this hyper-religious group of people to show us that man has a tendency to cloak his sinful nature in religious garb, to set up all kinds of rules and regulations, rights and wrongs, and religious rituals so that he can measure up to and thus earn his way into God's good favor. At the base of man's sinful nature is his tendency to become religious, to measure up, to earn his own way, to redeem himself by his own good, moral, religious behavior, to placate the Gods or God. We get a different picture when we read certain passages in both the Old and New Testaments: For "all our righteous deeds are like a polluted garment" (Is. 64:6) and "none is righteous, no, not one; no one understands, no one seeks for God" (Rom. 3:10).

What does this have to do with depression and false guilt? Just this: no person or no group—Christian or otherwise—is immune to Phariseeism. It is such a basic aspect of sin—this cloaking our sinful behavior in religious garb, this trying to earn our way into the favor of the Diety, this making of our own rules and regulations, that we never escape it.

As Pharisees, we have excelled at creating a pseudo righteousness for those of us who can measure up to our self-made rules—and false guilt for those who cannot. This yoke for the latter can become very, very depressing.

In theological terms we call this legalism. For many people it exacts a psychological toll resulting in some of life's most abysmal misery, hopelessness, pain, and depression. Compare this with the yoke of Christ, who says "my yoke is easy and my burden is light."

Legalism, of course, fails to see that it is not our faith which saves us, but the *object* of our faith. It is our faith in God which redeems us.

Look around you or within you and you will soon come upon someone or something who says this is the standard for a Christian. You must measure up to this. This is the behavior expected of a "real" Christian. (Are there *unreal* Christians?)

Christians Should Never Get Angry or Discouraged

The notion that a Christian should never feel angry or be discouraged can flood us with all kinds of false guilt if we really believe it. We can't live closely with others without getting angry from time to time. (I don't even believe we can live close to ourselves without getting angry once in a while.) Nor can we proceed through this life without periodic discouragement and even, at times, despair. That goes with living in a sinful environment or with our own sinful nature.

These unreal expectations may become very burdensome. Our Lord got angry and discouraged in His earthly ministry. Should we expect less? Should we demand of ourselves a standard even He didn't attain? With this mistaken notion we fail to see that both anger and discouragement are a realistic and even healthy part of life. Should we get discouraged when a church split occurs, disheartened when a close friend dies, dismayed when we catch the church treasurer filching from the missionary fund? Who wouldn't be both horribly angry and utterly destroyed to hear that his spouse is leaving him and the children for another woman? We must feel anger and discouragement to live in the real world. Nothing about Christianity exempts us from life (though some Christians try). This is not, of course, to say that anger and discouragement cannot lead to sin or be handled in sinful ways.

Archie comes to mind, a new minister in his second church. His first church experience had sent him up the wall. The board of elders constantly bickered. The leader of the women's group was a bull-headed, can't-take-no-for-an-answer sort of person who also insisted on being Sunday school superintendent. No one else really wanted the job, so it became hers by default. The youth leader did touchy-feely stuff with the young people's group which blew everybody's mind, and the church secretary was a gossip. Seminary hadn't prepared Archie for this. He was angry and discouraged, but in his thinking a minister should never feel that way, so he also felt horribly guilty for those feelings. He left the church after two years, and no one knew how he felt.

Now in this second parish it was happening again. Old Mr. McCurdy shot down every plan the new pastor came up with. Since McCurdy was a financial mainstay of the church, no one on the elder board would oppose him. Archie felt trapped, angry, discouraged, and, this time, depressed. Should he get out of the ministry, he asked me?

Archie felt very guilty for complaining about these people. A Christian shouldn't have these feelings, he emphasized, especially a minister. To identify that he did in fact have these feelings only made things worse. Knowing that he had them when he wasn't supposed to have them was itself most discouraging—another vicious circle. The more discouraged or angry he felt, the more he felt he ought not to feel that way, and this in turn made him more discouraged. Unfortunately, many things from Christian circles support this kind of "Thou shalt never be discouraged or angry" misconception that Archie struggled with.

Promises, Promises—and High Profits

You might hear a speaker or read a book suggesting a set of spiritual rules guaranteed to eliminate discouragement and turmoil. Don't believe it. There are no such

126

rules. Discouragement and turmoil are a part of life, and you can only escape these by trying to live in an unreal or make believe world or by living deceitfully and denying the reality of your situation.

I'm often amazed at the promises and claims made by the outside speaker who comes to town for a short series of meetings. He can promise the sky, give ten easy steps to the good life, and glibly tell you how to arrive. Then he leaves town and you never have the opportunity to watch him live day after day, or note the reactions of his intimates to him and how he treats them.

Your pastor, however, has to live with you the whole week after his sermon and week after week after that. He can't get out of town like the evangelist does. He can't just *tell* you as the outside speaker can; he also has to *show* you, and that's tough.

I for one am weary of all the hoopla accorded in some circles to the "outside speaker." I'm tired of the acclaim and adoration we bestow upon flashy personalities who tell us where we should be and give ten easy steps and the techniques to get there. They promise a lot but they don't have to deliver. They dump their standards for living on us, then move on to the next town. Unlike the local minister, they don't stay around to live out the message they proclaim. Your pastor can't get away with that.

When I first came to Ohio from California it startled me to find a speaker there from California. He was greatly respected in Ohio, but no one had heard of him back home. I also know of a speaker from Ohio who makes only small waves at home but a big splash in other parts of the country.

A writer is in the same position. You never get to live with him to see if what he tells you to do actually works for him. In his book he may tell you how magnificently everything worked out for him, but I say, don't tell me,

127

show me. Don't try to substitute personality or charisma for godliness. Unfortunately this happens all too often in evangelical circles. (This may be why so many local ministers appear to be lackluster, dull personalities. We compare them with the authors and renowned speakers who appear so glamorous. In reality they're much like ourselves.)

I want to apply this to the world of pop psychology where all kinds of gurus currently are running around the country with formulas and promises for the good life, serene marriage, sexual bliss, peace of mind, or emotional ecstasy. Evangelicals or religionists have no exclusive claims to such a phenomenon. Medicine men we shall always have with us, peddling their elixirs of the good life for a price. It used to come in bottles. Today we can find it in weekend workshops, seminars, and taped cassettes.

Untempted Christian?

The Pharisees commonly preach another mistaken notion of the Christian life: the idea that a Christian should have no desire to sin. Those who believe this may be caught in another vicious circle that leads to depression. I once heard a speaker say that some people don't sin nor are they tempted to sin because they are too old, too ugly, or too poor. That may be crude, but it still says something important. Some people aren't tempted in some areas for the simple reason that the opportunity to sin is not there for them.

This notion completely misses the clearly biblical concept that temptation itself is not sin. Sin comes in the way we respond to temptation, whether or not we yield to it. Our Lord was "tempted in all points like as we are, yet without sin." Many of us understand that in our head but not in our gut, therefore, we feel guilty even when we're absolutely convinced we're not guilty. It's important to realize here that it is not feelings of guilt that establish whether or not we really are guilty. As we said before, we can feel guilty without having violated God's laws because of false standards we've adopted. And we can violate God's laws without feeling guilty, because we've redefined sin to exclude our own behavior. The guilt we feel is too closely determined by our consciences, which is in turn determined by our background. It is shaped by man, not necessarily by God.

Past Sinful Effects Eliminated?

Another misconception of the Christian faith promises that becoming a Christian will eliminate the *consequences* of past sins and that painful memories or remnants of past sins will be expulsed forever. Not only is this not true, but again it sets us up for depression. If you are an alcoholic, becoming a Christian won't automatically change that. You have a resource to overcome that alcoholism that you didn't have before, but your new spiritual condition doesn't change your physical condition. God will not restore you to your previous condition because you have become a Christian. If you have suffered the long-term effects of venereal disease (even brain damage is possible), don't expect that finding faith will restore your lost physical or mental skills.

We cannot violate the natural laws of God without suffering the consequences. If you, in callous disregard of safe-driving requirements, take the life of another, that life cannot be restored nor can the pain in your soul be forgotten. God removes our past transgressions as far as the "east is from the west." He deals with our sins, pays the price, but we can't forget them. We need not feel condemned, but we may still feel badly as that memory returns.

Unfortunately, when those memories return, some people feel that God has not forgiven them. They then feel they must abuse themselves or punish themselves mercilessly and endlessly. This masochistic behavior leads to hopelessness, despair, and depression. This happens more often where people are led to believe that conversion completely eradicates the results of past sins.

Christians Don't Doubt

A Christian who lives a life of obedience should never doubt according to the pharisees. And this expectation also leads to false guilt which leads to depression. But it doesn't work that way. We all doubt. Faith itself is fashioned in the workshop of doubt. If we grow in faith it will be because we have dared to doubt, have asked the hard questions, have struggled with our lack of faith and pressed these concerns to God Himself. Job did; David did; Thomas did. Shouldn't we?

Easy believism and bumper-sticker mentalities tell us that "Christ is the answer," but they sell short the profundity of the Christian faith, its message and ultimate answer to life.

Believing is not easy at all; it's tough. We do an injustice to people, to the problem of sin, and to the Christian faith when we make it sound easy. We are unfair to believers to make them believe that once they have accepted Christ as Savior they should have no more doubts.

Look at John the Baptist. In fiery language he proclaimed to all that the Messiah had come. He was the first one to point people to Jesus as the "One who was to come." Later in his life, however, in prison, John had deep doubts about the very message he himself had so fiercely proclaimed in public. Jesus had just not turned out as he had expected, and John wondered if He were really the Messiah. He wanted more evidence. He believed, yes; but he doubted, too.

"I believe, help Thou mine unbelief" epitomizes honest faith. Can we do more? To believe that doubts indicate a lack of faith completely misses the difference between doubting and unbelief. When we equate these two, we fail to acknowledge that doubting is a prerequisite to faith. We can't increase faith unless we deal with and face the hard issues of belief.

Don't let those Pharisees get you down. Your doubting is not evidence of unbelief, and it may lead to greater faith. Besides you can't just pretend those doubts aren't there. Rather than get worked up over the fact that you're doubting, look them full in the face. Go search for some answers, but don't expect them on a silver platter personally delivered to your door. It doesn't work that way.

Christians Don't Have Emotional Problems

Another pharisaical standard that can get you feeling guilty is the idea that a Christian who lives a life of obedience to God will never experience emotional problems. This one is in the same class as the one we have already discussed—that Christians should never be angry or discouraged. The same observations apply here.

The story of Job is relevant here. The pharisees with whom Job dealt were convinced that if you prospered you were right with God, if you suffered adversity it was because you were not right with God. The Book of Job makes clear to us that this is *not* the way it is. Many problems, including emotional problems, are not necessarily the result of our own behavior. Some are; some are not.

Related to this is the "suffering servant" concept of Scripture. Part of our own redemptive ministry in this world will involve some suffering on our part. "For it has been granted to you that for the sake of Christ you should not only believe in Him but also suffer for his sake" (Phil. 1:29). If we are to "weep with those who weep" and "mourn with those who mourn," it will entail suffering for us as well. The ability to help another is oft times related to having experienced that problem ourselves. It is most reassuring to some persons in the throes of a depression to hear that someone else has been there and has made it through to a brighter side. That can really help.

Guilt for Being Human

In the chapter on anger, we said that ambivalence in human relations is normal. We can't live closely with another human being without having both positive and negative feelings toward them. We're like porcupines; the closer we get the warmer it is, but the more it hurts. This fits our Christian belief that man is a sinner, and the closer we get to one another the more those sinful aspects of ourselves will show.

Unfortunately we will always have pharisees around us who fail to see the ambivalences of life—they can't accept that love is mixed with hurt, faith with doubt, hope with despair, and joy with sorrow. So they inform us that God would not have it this way, that we should, for example, never have any feelings of anger or dislike for our parents, spouse or children. If old Mr. McCurdy bugs us, they tell us we're not being Christian.

Frequently a depressed young mother shows up in my

office. She is right in the middle of diapers, struggling with the terrible twos, fighting the confinement of a small house, listening to demands of infants. By the time the kids are finally in bed she's exhausted, and then, totally wiped out, she has to face the sexual demands of an anything but an exhausted husband. By this time, she is too tired and emotionally drained to even think of sex. She is very ambivalent toward her husband—angry at him for not helping her more, sympathetic with his sexual needs, and mad at herself for being so tired.

But what really gets to her is her anger at her children. How can she love her children so very much and still get so angry at them, even feel that she doesn't like them at times. What kind of a Christian is she? How could she be this way? In fact, the reason she came in is that just last Tuesday she found herself literally screaming at Todd after he had dumped his oatmeal all over the baby. Then there was the time Tom announced he was going to join a third softball team, and she just hated him for that. He already played on the church team, and on the one at work. But Christians shouldn't have feelings of hate, she felt, and Tom had told her it was such an opportunity for him to witness to his faith. So all these negative feelings which she felt Christians weren't supposed to have increased and drove her to depression.

How sad! Who had the audacity to tell this young mother that she should have only positive feelings for her children and husband? Who led her to believe that as a Christian she shouldn't feel anger toward her husband. Why, I'm angry at Tom just hearing about him, the insensitive, selfish clod!

Mixed feelings toward our children or our spouses are not wrong. They are inevitable. I remember a time when we couldn't find my son who was then about three. We had told him he could play with friends in a certain area, but he wasn't there nor anywhere we looked. I combed the area without success. I thought of the river that ran through our neighborhood. It's not a big one, but the last spring a two-year-old had drowned in it. Panic struck me. The river was very high now, and I imagined his body floating down the river face down. My wife was out searching, too, when I spied him coming out of a new neighbor's basement, pleased with himself for having met a new friend and being invited in. I was fantastically relieved and furious with him all at once. With tears of joy in my eyes and angry words on my tongue (Where have you been? Why didn't you tell mother?), I engulfed him in my arms. I was mad at him and ecstatic at his well being, all at once. Mixed feelings, even contradictory feelings, are part of human relationships.

Have you ever sat at home waiting for a husband or wife or teenage child who was out later at night than you had expected? You worried about them and imagined terrible things happening. Then they came in all bubbly and enthusiastic, having had a good time? You were relieved, yes, but offended, too, for here you had been sweating it out and meanwhile they'd just been enjoying themselves. Talk about ambivalence! Should we feel guilty for these mixed feelings? Hardly! Foolish, perhaps, but not guilty.

People often ask in counseling, how is it that I can feel this way and that way, too? Isn't there something wrong? I can't both like and dislike, love and hate my children, my spouse, my parents, can I? Then we have the Christian who, following some fateful tragedy in his life, struggles with God for allowing this to have occurred. He has angry feelings for God, and this leaves him feeling guilty. If parents feel that they can't be angry at God, that they can't express their hurt and confusion, it can be very depressing. As we said before, the Psalmist rails at God for many things he sees that make him angry at God. Job, too, expresses his acute displeasure at God for letting all these tragedies occur. Don't worry. God can take it. He will even understand.

Sex Guilt

Most marriage counselors have seen this. A young couple recently married comes in quite upset, somewhat beside themselves. She has horrible feelings of guilt and dirtiness about sexual intercourse. She may even feel guilty for removing her clothes. In fact, she can't, so she does it under the covers or attempts intercourse partially clothed. Because of these guilty feelings she resists the whole business. Or she does it but feels miserable afterwards. Sometimes it is the male who has this problem.

There again we find false guilt at play. They know in their heads that there is nothing wrong, but that doesn't change their feelings. In the process of growing up their emotions regarding sex had been shaped by pharisaical overkill. They had learned from parents, perhaps from church, that sex was wrong.

Victorious Christian Living

One of the more deadly and depressing gambits pharisees pull on us is the "top of the mountain" myth. If you're really a committed Christian, you won't have ups and downs in your Christian life. It will all be up. You will live victoriously on the mountain top. Whole movements in Christianity have based themselves on this yearning for a stable spiritual life.

Many spend a lifetime following this will-o'-the-wisp. They attend meetings, conferences, travel here and there, spend their hard-earned cash for books and tapes.

135

They buy into one of these movements after another. Enthusiastic at first, absolutely convinced and firmly committed, they involve others. Then it fades; their enthusiasm wanes, and a few years later they choose another movement. After such a burst of fervor, they blame themselves for having fallen back into lukewarmness. After achieving great victories of obedience, they become dismayed to find new sins slithering around unconquered.

We need a larger perspective. We need to see that there can be no mountain peaks if there are no valleys. There can be no victories if there are no struggles. Think of the irrational and illogical nature of promising a constantly victorious existence that would not involve struggles. What would you then have victory over?

Our relationship with God is never on a straight plain. Instead it involves a long succession of returning to the path that leads to Him. As I move closer to God, a Holy God, I will become increasingly aware of sins that I was not previously aware of. With awareness, then comes a struggle. Just becoming aware of them doesn't mean they're conquered. So there will also be some defeats.

You see then that the closer I get to God, the more up and down my spiritual life may seem. Some will hear me saying that one *should* sin "that grace may abound." Paul has already spoken to that point. It's not that you *should* sin, but that you *will* sin. And as you move closer to God you will only increase in the awareness of sin in your life. And that can go on till you die.

The only people I know with a stable spiritual existence are those who, in the guise of holiness, have successfully repressed and denied to themselves their own sinful tendencies. They've pulled the wool over their own eyes and thus have suppressed their sinful awareness.

This frenetic search for a perfect anything inevitably

dooms one to frustration and despair. Nothing is sadder to see than a holiness seeker who has thrown in the towel. We can't help but feel sympathy for them, for they have often been victims of religious systems which promised more than they could deliver.

Right now this same dynamic is occurring in the secular world in massive proportions. There are all kinds of gurus promising a life of happiness and peace of mind if one will only attend the workshops, buy the books, listen to the tapes, follow the techniques, etc. But just as in the religious world, they promise more than they can deliver.

All of these movements, religious and secular, try to market full-time happiness. They want you to believe that you can come to the place emotionally or spiritually where there are no ups and downs and where bliss or achievement is a constant of life. They fail to see that happiness and spiritual well-being are both *by-products* of what you do. They cannot be sought in their own right. We'll be happy only when we're doing those things that are accompanied by happiness—living the good life, caring for others, trying out something new, etc., etc. And in the spiritual world we'll experience well-being and contentment only when we have done the will of God— which is "to do justice, and kindness, to love and to walk humbly with your God" (Mic. 6:8). Get yourself to do those things and you will experience happiness and God's peace. The problem is to be that consistent in one's walk. It's not tough to find, but it is tough to do.

CHAPTER VIII

THE DEPRESSIVE EFFECTS
OF PHARISEEISM

WE HAVE JUST DESCRIBED a number of ways in which man-made religious laws produce false guilt and depression in our lives. We have seen how the ever-present pharisees make us feel guilty for not measuring up to their arbitrary standards or burden us with expectations that go beyond those we find in the Bible. Now we have to ask, what happens to people who accept these other-imposed norms and beliefs and try to meet these expectations? What psychological and spiritual consequences must they face?

Deceit

If someone is constantly concerned about whether or not others approve of his behavior, there is a danger that he will start to live deceitfully. He may come to have two existences—the image he projects to the Christian world and the reality inside. He may be what James calls the "doubleminded man who is unstable in all his ways." He will play the role of having arrived, or meeting the expectations, but it's all a front, an attempt to appear more spiritual than he is. Add to this the frightening possibility that he not only lives a lie, but he may believe it himself. We call the psychological mechanism involved here "denial."

138

Denial

Now this gets scary, for if someone actually believes that he is somewhere spiritually or emotionally where he is not, he will come to the point where he can't even see for himself what is happening. He can't be convicted or corrected because he feels that any advice or observations about his behavior don't even apply to him.

Most Christians who come to this point generally are not guilty of gross sins, and this makes it more deceptive. They can easily cloak whatever sins they have in religious garb, or cover them with the garments of self-righteousness. What appears to be devoutness or piety *may actually be sin*. This, of course, describes the condition of the Pharisees of Scripture. They sinned in the very acts they thought were marks of devotion and piety.

Persons guilty of more gross sins can't pull this off so easily. The prostitute, for example, can't easily think of her act as religious devotion. The armed robber can't claim that he is living up to God's expectations. In this sense, then, of the awareness of sin, the prostitute and the robber are often one step closer to finding the kingdom of God than is the Pharisee.

Seared Consciences and Hardened Hearts

Trying to live up to the unreal expectations of the Pharisees may result in a seared conscience. (This may be the next step beyond denial.) The person who works hard to attain these man-made religious expectations, has no time or effort left to meet God's expectations. For example, he may feel horribly guilty for missing a Bible study or a mid-week church service, but feel nothing for injustice done to an employee. He may feel engulfed with guilt for even thinking of drinking or smoking, but have no qualms whatever about gossip or envy.

This denial syndrome often forces the Pharisees to define sin very narrowly. They list such things as swearing, drinking, smoking, not tithing or not having daily Bible study, but they completely overlook such weightier matters as deceit, injustice, and materialism. They define sin to include only those evils of which they are *already not guilty* or where they already measure up. Sin by definition becomes those evils of which others are guilty. How many Christians do you suppose still have no conscience in areas of social ethics, in spite of their devotion to the Bible which clearly denounces social injustice. Because they have so effectively redefined sin and narrowed it down to a size that leaves them guiltless, they can read these passages without making the obvious applications to their own world. The Bible refers to the "hardened heart," and we usually think of this as someone who has fallen to the utter depths of sin. However, I think we should apply it to those who have used religion to deceive themselves into thinking they are the true believers.

Projection

Redefining sin as the other guy's problem causes the Pharisees to be very preoccupied with the sins of "the world." By focusing on the so-called wrongdoing of others, they remain blind to their own transgressions and ungodly Phariseeism. By constantly clucking about sins for which they are not guilty, they convince themselves that they are God's chosen few. This creates an illusion of superiority. In group therapy sessions I've observed a number of such people with holier-than-thou attitudes. They roundly and soundly condemn other group members, but simply can't see their own sinful behavior no matter how obvious it was to everyone else in the group.

That same behavior was frequently the source of their emotional disturbance.

I'll never forget Myra. She had been hospitalized many times for severe depression. She had received shock treatments, drugs, all kinds of medications—everything there was to give. After a short time in the group, she let one woman know, in no uncertain terms, that she was living in sin. The woman had been twice divorced. She chewed up another member for her excessive make-up, and condemned one more for having a child out of wedlock. Almost everyone she judged for failure to attend church. Before long the group picked up on this ever-present hostility and hatred that dominated Myra's life. She had a thousand hostile complaints about her husband. She had a whole host of hostilities for the many doctors she had ever seen. She had burnt anyone who had ever gotten close to her, especially those who had tried to help. At first, whenever someone tried to help her she would sing their praises. Sooner or later, however, usually sooner, that appreciation cooled and turned to hatred and icy contempt. The whole world could see this chronic hostility of Myra's, *except Myra*. She was so busy chewing out and focusing on the sinnerhood of everyone else, she couldn't see what the world could clearly see—that hostility was ripping her apart. Her preoccupation with tearing down sinners was an unconscious means of coping with her own failure to arrive and measure up. When a person feels secure in the love of God, he is notably forgiving as well as tolerant of others. Myra lacked this security.

One time my wife attended a series of home Bible studies which she found quite unsatisfying. As she tried to put her finger on the problem, she realized that the people were using Scripture solely as a launching pad to denounce all the evils in the world around them and to

141

cluck about the bad behavior of others, especially other church groups. This preoccupation with the other group's supposed sin, helped them effectively evade God's message in Scripture for themselves. When they got through they felt very devout and good about one another and above criticism. Why, they have just been studying the Bible—who could criticize that! Again we see a cloaking of sinful behavior in religious garb with its unlimited potential for self-deception and denial. How tragic!

This tendency to focus on the sins of the other guy sometimes leads us to usurp the work of the Holy Spirit. We begin to monitor the lives of others and take upon ourselves the responsibility of convicting them of sin. Not only do we play God, we even try to outgod God. We go beyond what the God of Scripture does by trying to force on others our condemnation and conviction, thus violating their God-given free wills.

Psychosomatic Ills

One result of such deceit and denial is physiological tension symptoms and psychosomatic disorders. I wouldn't want to say without proof that Christians suffer from more psychosomatic disorders than non-Christians, but I wouldn't be surprised if it were true, especially with evangelical Christians. I'd like to see some research here as well as some possible explanations.

One explanation could be the difficulty many Christians have acknowledging emotional problems. They feel that Christians aren't supposed to have such problems. Christians should be "anxious for nothing," they should "rest in God," experience "perfect peace" with "minds stayed on Thee." So when emotional distress occurs, rather than dealing with it directly, they sweep it under the rug (which psychologically means they turn the distress into their bodies rather than deal with their emotions at the emotional level). That, of course, would blow their cover of having it all together, of being A-1 Christians. Instead they cultivate ulcers, precipitate migraine headaches, break out in skin disorders, have "these terrible headaches" or chronic lower back pain or the hundred and one other physical symptoms that are either aggravated or precipitated by undercover emotional distress.

Fear

Where acceptance and approval depends on measuring up to certain standards, we must constantly guard areas in our own lives that don't come up to these standards. We can't tell the truth about ourselves for fear that we will be rejected and condemned by those whose approval we need. Even our own approval of ourselves may be at stake.

Cindy knew that her dad and mom did not approve of her behavior. Nor did the other people in the church for that matter. Nor did God, she thought. As far back as she could remember, her folks hassled her about not measuring up, about not behaving like a good Christian and minister's daughter should.

It appeared to Cindy that her parents thought her brother, David, three years older, was perfect. He always seemed to please them. He never made waves and never rebelled as Cindy did. (And chronically wanted to). He did all the church things, went to all the services, never complained. He participated in all the young people's activities and was a leader for this and that. Now he was in school, planning to be a minister.

Cindy, on the other hand, had often refused to attend

143

church services. One time she had even tried to avoid Sunday morning service, and Dad had gotten so angry he lost control and hit her with his open hand across the face. She had gone but totally against her will. It made her furious to hear her father preach that morning as though nothing had happened.

Her parents also forced her to say she was sorry and to ask God's forgiveness, whether she wanted to or not. It was so maddening to have to stand there and say "I'm sorry" to Dave or Mother when she wasn't in the least bit sorry. But if she didn't say it and didn't mouth a prayer asking God's forgiveness, she would incur Dad's wrath and his rejection, plus an endless sermon on how disappointed God was with her.

Whenever Mother got sick (she was always getting sick), it was Cindy's fault. Cindy upset her, her father would say. Mother was always hurt by the way Cindy acted or by something she had said or had failed to do.

Then there was the "what are people going to think?" and "what are the people in church going to say?" argument. Many times they inferred that Cindy would be responsible for Dad having to leave the church, maybe even ruin his ministry if she didn't shape up.

One time they found cigarettes in her purse. Mother often searched her purse, Cindy knew that, but still she left them there. She didn't know why and supposed it was kind of dumb. She could have gotten rid of them, but for some strange reason she hoped Mother would find them. Cindy came home after school that day to find Dad enraged and Mother sobbing. Dad screamed and yelled for almost two hours. How could she do this to them? Was she demon-possessed? Had her testimony last Sunday night been all a hoax? Had she no respect for her parents at all? She just couldn't keep betraying God again and again and expect Him to forgive her forever. She had hurt them deeply. (They looked more angry than hurt.) Finally, they all had to get on their knees and pray. Dad prayed that Cindy would come to see how she had "grieved the Holy Spirit," that she would end up some horrible person if she didn't change the direction she was going, that "God cast out this demon of rebelliousness" in her. Cindy could have puked. He wasn't praying to God at all. He was still preaching to her. Mother got sick that evening and for most of that next week.

Another time a guy at school had asked her out, and when she asked Dad if she could go, it was like the inquisition. Dad called the minister of the church where Gordy attended and asked about Gordy and his folks. Later Dad drove Cindy by Gordy's parents' home. (She didn't know how Dad found out where Gordy lived.) It was a dumpy house, and Dad wanted to know if that's the kind of house she wanted to live in. She hadn't even dated him once, yet her dad had her married off. The verdict came a few days later. No, Cindy couldn't go with Gordy. It wouldn't be the kind of relationship in which a Christian girl should involve herself.

These were some of the stories that emerged as Cindy talked. She came to me because she had recently threatened suicide. That did it. Her parents panicked. Cindy would have to get professional help. Why, imagine what people at church would say if something serious had happened, if this had become public information. They had heard I was a Christian, so they wanted me to counsel Cindy. But was I a "born-again Christian" they asked? (I felt like saying I didn't know of any other kind, but resisted.) Now I should be alert, they informed me, to the fact that demon possession might be involved here. After all, there was no other reason for her to act this way. Heaven knows they had brought her up in a Christian home with all the Christian love and concern possible. It was not likely anything they had done, they observed, just look how fine Dave had turned out, and both children had been treated the same.

By now Cindy was quite depressed. She was twenty and still living at home. She had no self-confidence, no self-esteem, only self-loathing and self-condemnation. She felt condemned by her parents, her brother, her church, and God. She had spent much of her life fluctuating between two poles. She would feel like a very bad person for some reason or another, for something she had thought or done. Then she would "come back" to God and ask for forgiveness. But it wouldn't be long before she'd do something "bad" again, like not having a daily quiet time or refusing to attend a church service. Then every so often she had this urge to *really* do something like smoking those cigarettes, some rebellious act. Actually she had never smoked in public (though her folks didn't believe that). She was always alone. It just felt good, kind of fun, free-like. But she always felt when she did these things that it was wrong and that not only her parents but God, too, disapproved. Cindy was a very guilty person. She had eventually come to the point where she felt guilty for living.

When her father developed cancer she knew that that was God's wrath for all the bad things she had done. She felt very guilty and responsible for that. God was punishing her, she knew it. Her mother faced serious surgery on her leg with the probability of not walking right again, and Cindy knew that, too, was all her fault. She had heard it so many times she believed it herself. Where do you turn when even God condemns you? Poor Cindy! She was in many ways a victim of a sinful, self-righteous religious system, but because this sinful family system of pride, hostility, and self-righteousness was cloaked in the garments of evangelical religion, it left Cindy without

146

recourse. To oppose her parents was to oppose God. Her parents certainly never questioned that. They could never see that Cindy's rebellions were a direct result of their own bad behavior.

The Slough of Despond

A vicious circle operates for many who, like Cindy, try to live up to pharisee-imposed standards. In trying to meet these standards, they see more imperfection in themselves and become even more vulnerable to guilt feelings and depression. Their depression results in a lack of motivation and energy to expend in meeting the standards. Like the child raised in a home of impossibly high achievement standards, they eventually either give up and quit trying or rebel and chuck the standards completely.

Also, if they try to repress the anger they are bound to feel, they end up committing such a large proportion of psychic energy to that repression that they don't have any left over for profitable things. They get exhausted trying to keep their anger down. They have no energy left for activities that produce positive rewards for them.

Cindy couldn't afford to be angry with her parents because they were the reinforcements for her. She walked a tight rope of wanting desperately to strike back at them and at the same time realizing that that could remove her one positive reinforcement in life.

Rebellion

A pharisaical regime of arbitrarily chosen and arbitrarily imposed standards will result in rebellion. Many individuals caught in such a trap, especially late adolescents, will simply break out and throw off the shackles of these standards. As a result, they will likely prevent the possibility of depression. They may have other problems, however. The person who, inside, still adheres to these imposed values is a more likely candidate for depression. Because depression is not as likely in those who rebel, we will only mention this response in passing as a very common effect and outcome of phariseeism. It's worth a book all its own and we can't do justice to it here.

I hope you don't hear me condoning rebellion in youth. Sometimes it is good and necessary, in fact essential, but in other cases rebellion can be downright sinful and abhorrent. We are not here dealing with rebellion, but with the phariseeism which precipitates it. Rebellion is like anger; one can express it in constructive or destructive ways. Remember "be angry and sin not"? It's the same with rebellion.

Teaching in a Christian college I see a lot of struggles with rebellion and depression in response to parentally imposed standards. The youth who seems to hurt the most is the one who, like Cindy, rebels in part or periodically. He has so absorbed the standards, however, that he never really evaluates them. He alternates between rebellion and depression. He is not free. He is periodically overwhelmed with guilt and exceedingly repentant at such times. At other times he can't wait to burst the bonds that hold him. Such young people become suckers for the overpowering tin-pan-alley teams (frequently singing groups) that tour the evangelical college circuit. Their Hollywood style and method appeal to youth, but the conviction of sin they try to arouse comes from playing on these gut-level standards. It's like the wolf in sheep's clothing for these youths. They respond to the appeal and later find they're struggling with the same old problems. The commitment doesn't last, but the evangelistic group leaves town with a beautiful tally of responses to include in their promotional literature. How much preferable (and more ethical) is the appeal which gets young people to *evaluate* their gut-level standards, to compare them to scriptual guidelines, and to encourage them to make a free commitment to values they can then call their own. (This lack of ethics in so much of evangelism is depressing in itself.)

Self-Punishment

Many respond to phariseeism by becoming self-punitive. As in the case of introverted hostility that we discussed in the chapter on anger (where anger turns inward against the self), these people try to punish themselves for failure to live up to these standards. They seek forgiveness for not measuring up by punishing themselves. If I really downgrade myself, or make things difficult for me, or put myself down, or literally punish myself, perhaps I will deserve to feel okay.

We can easily see how this can come about. As children we have probably all learned to associate feelings of guilt and punishment. A child may, in fact, learn to believe that punishment is *required* to get Mother or Dad's forgiveness. That's the usual sequence that leads to forgiveness, anyway. Thus, later in life when feeling guilty, we may seek punishment to feel forgiven. And if we live in a guilt-inducing setting or have ourselves absorbed impossible standards, then we feel a constant need to either seek out punishment or to punish ourselves. We respond to guilt automatically by seeking punishment.

I have seen some of these individuals who, as a result, are the most intense, driving, and perfectionistic persons possible. They may be, for example, some of the hardest working people in the church. The problem, of course, is that they are motivated by fear, and their work is an attempt to atone for guilt. There is a depressive aura to them and to all their diligence rather than the enthusiasm of honest commitment. It's something they *have* to do, or else they'll feel guilty.

As we said in the chapter on anger, a Freudian view suggests that shock treatments act as a form of punishment which the depressive needs to relieve guilty feelings. That's a highly debatable explanation, but there is no doubt that many depressives punish themselves.

How much better is the biblical concept of forgiveness, which is based on reconciliation rather than a punitive model of forgiveness. Rather than trying to placate our consciences by punishing ourselves, we can accept the reconciliation already provided in Christ. From this position of being forgiven and accepted, we can then move on to be agents of reconciliation to others. Punishment is useless, and the remorse that accompanies it is depressing.

You see, there's an interesting kind of pride involved in self-punishment. We try to earn the right to be forgiven. Then if we have earned it, why, of course, we deserve it. So it ends up not being forgiveness at all. We can't erase the effect of most of our sins and crimes. We can only deal with sin by being forgiven, accepting it, and working at reconciling ourselves to a new way of behaving.

Self-Punishment Expected by Others

Sometimes I have seen spouses demand that their partners punish themselves to earn their forgiveness for some offense committed against them. The usual story involves unfaithfulness. The faithful spouse expects the wayward one to demonstrate a lot of self-punishment to be restored to the innocent spouse's good favor.

I remember a pastor's wife who said she had forgiven her husband for that affair back in their church fourteen years ago. However, she went into such detail about the great injustice against her, I suspected otherwise. Also, she repeatedly insisted that she had forgiven him, and I wondered who she was trying to convince. Certainly she had been hurt and deeply so, but could she never work it through? No, probably not as long as she kept insisting that he must continue to punish himself for this bad behavior. In almost devious ways, she could make him feel guilty and force him to punish himself for the injustice he had wrought in her life. She even had a way of attributing certain physical ills to this event. Only when he would punish himself in some way or once again beg her for forgiveness, could he find peace.

I know of another similar case where the wife went into chronic angry depression following an episode of unfaithfulness by her husband. For many years thereafter she seemed to delight in making his life as miserable as possible. She frequently threatened suicide and attributed her depression to "what he had done to her" back then. She was happy only when she could get him to punish himself. She had an uncanny ability to make all the adversities of their lives attributable to this unfaithfulness. She became a semi-invalid, forcing him to wait on her and to do household tasks that she just "wasn't able to do anymore." Her physical ills looked hypochondriacal to me as well as to the umpteen physicians she had sought out, most of whom could find no physical basis for her complaints.

Acknowledgement of Sinnerhood

Before we leave this chapter, I'd like to suggest a basic Christian principle that, if incorporated into our lives,

can go a long way toward helping us to evade the consequences and effects of phariseeism. That principle is
simply the awareness of our own sinnerhood, our sinful
past, our current struggle with sin, and our unlimited
potential for sin. We need to have this awareness at the
forefront of our minds all the days of our lives. We're still
creatures, not creators. We are sinners, even though
saved. We're *not* restored angels. We are still on the
journey; we have not yet arrived.

It is a matter of simple honesty. If we acknowledge
where we really stand in the light of God's laws, we realize
we all have miles of light years yet to travel. Only by
massive deception of ourselves as well as with others can
we pretend to have arrived, to be already Christ-like.

How sad that all around us churches have inculcated
into their very existence the mechanics that allow this
massive self-deception and denial to go on unchallenged
by either God's Word or the Christian's own heart. That,
I am convinced, is one of the saddest stories of Christen-
dom. Many of those who talk the most about sin (the
other guy's) are often the guiltiest in this regard. If we are
truly honest with ourselves, we shall have no difficulty at
all in discovering reasons for humbling ourselves. And,
thank God, to acknowledge our sinnerhood *given His
grace* is to move toward wholeness.

CHAPTER IX

GUILT AND DEPRESSION: REAL GUILT

I AM CONVINCED that one of the major causes of depression is sinful behavior. I have seen it time and time again. So much so that as a therapist I must consider this as an explanation along with other possible causes. I have learned that the hard way.

I have often worked for months with individuals who have had all kinds of depressive and neurotic symptoms and with whom I made little progress until it came out that they had been conscience-stricken over some waywardness. I have seen the whole gamut of emotional disorders displayed as a result of sinful behavior. Their symptoms may have no connection whatever with their bad behavior, except to indicate tension and stress.

Many times I've worked with clients who have seen other therapists for their depression but had not come to grips with this possible causative factor. When they did face this possible cause, the depression often lifted quickly. I have also seen numerous cases where the issue of the conscience-stricken behavior did come up for discussion but was not considered a problem by the therapist. It was left unattended, and the depression was left unresolved.

153

Sin, the Cause

Sharon is a good example. She was the wife of a young attorney who was making quite a name for himself in the community. Life had consisted of a round of social events and community activities with Sharon. She was active in the attorneys' wives' organization and had served as chairperson of numerous committees and at one point the chief organizer of an annual gala affair.

She came to see me, however, in the middle of deep depression. She was absolutely miserable, had no energy whatsoever, had dropped out of every activity and responsibility she had previously been involved in, and was unable to attend to even the simplest of responsibilities at home. No one could believe the change in Sharon. She had lost weight. She couldn't sleep. She had no appetite. She found it difficult to even dress herself properly (though previously known as a sharp dresser). If her mother hadn't stepped in to help, the home would have been total chaos.

In getting background information on Sharon, I found that she had had a depressive episode earlier in her marriage. Immediately following the birth of their first child, Sharon had gone into a depression that was diagnosed as a post-partum depression by a psychiatrist. She had been unable to function with the new baby. This, of course, would be a logical diagnosis under the circumstances. A post-partum depression follows childbirth and is thought to be due to chemical changes.

A vastly different explanation, however, emerged from our discussions. Sharon didn't need to refer to any hormonal changes to account for her supposedly post-partum depression. She had been having an affair with another young attorney, a friend and sometime colleague of her husband. Soon after arriving home with the new baby, she had had sexual intercourse in her own home with this paramour. As she said it "with my very own baby asleep right next to us." She had tried to break off the affair when she had become pregnant, and this was the first time they had gotten together since then. It overwhelmed her and she felt very guilty and became deeply depressed.

Now her doctor, knowing of her supposedly post-partum depression, believed this second depression to be an endogenous (internally caused) depression. I learned, however, that her affair with this other man was still going on.

Sharon's guilt and bad feelings about herself had caught up with her. The deceit with her husband, the lies, the attempts to cover up, her own lack of sexual response to her husband—all these came to a head in emotional exhaustion and depression. Ironically, the other attorney's wife kept crying on Sharon's shoulder about her marriage. Sharon's life was so tense and intolerable, the conflicting demands so overwhelming, that it all collapsed around her.

Once this had all been faced and dealt with (it wasn't easy), the guilt removed, commitments renewed, Sharon's vivaciousness returned and she had a new lease on life and her marriage. Oh, lots of things had to be worked out in the marriage, but they both pursued that in a way that made their marriage better than it had been before.

Moralistic?

The notion that sin can cause depression will offend some and appear simplistic. They may also take offense at the use of the word sin. It sounds too puritanical, old-fashioned, and moralistic to many in the mental health field. But we can dismiss sin as a cause of emotional disturbance only at great peril to the continued mental health and well being of the client. In many cases we simply can't make significant progress without coming to grips with this dimension. Dr. Karl Menninger faced this in his recent book, *What Ever Became of Sin?* I highly recommend this book. It is a sage attempt to reintroduce into our society's thinking the possibility of sinful behavior as one of the major causes of emotional problems and mental disorder.

Sin by Whose Standards?

I make no apologies for using the word sin. The straightforward use of this word does not imply moralism or puritanism. The problem of course is that few in our modern world agree on what sin is. (I have found that no matter how diverse views are at the head level, there is much greater agreement at the gut level. People frequently hurt inside, even when they violate values they repudiate in their head.)

Christians, of course, view sin as the violation of the standards that God has given us in Scripture. Non-Christians may not adhere to nor accept these standards. That is their God-given right. So then, what does sin refer to for them? I think every man has a sense of "ought." He feels he must perform certain acts and not do others. These are his values, though they may not agree with someone else's. If he violates any of his values, he will likely experience dissonance between what he's doing and what he values. This dissonance is experienced as guilt.

If people do not live up to their own values, they open themselves up to all kinds of problems, including emotional problems, especially depression. Therefore, a psychotherapist must check to see if the person is in fact

156

living in violation of his own values. (This need not involve a value judgment on the part of the therapist.) He needs to find out if the symptoms are an expression of this form of dissonance in the person's life.

Sin Without Guilt?

The question then arises, what if someone violates a standard of God which is not a standard in this person's own value system? Will he still experience guilt? I don't pretend to have a nicely tied up answer to that question. It is, in fact, a very big question. No doubt some people violate what I consider to be God's law, but they experience no guilt. I think we can go further than that. Some people break laws all Christians would subscribe to, but they experience *no* guilt. I do believe that whether or not they feel guilty for such a violation of God's laws or standards, they still experience problems in their life as a result of this violation. You can't go against the grain of the universe and not get splinters. It won't work. You will experience some negative results whether you feel guilty or not.

I remember a young man who had broken at least one or two of the ten commandments every week he came to see me. Though married, he was "sleeping around" a couple of nights every week, for example. He incessantly stole from his employees. Guilty? No matter how hard you looked, you couldn't detect the slightest trace of guilt. (We refer to this kind of person in the mental health field as a psychopathic personality. They have sometimes been described as "a man without a conscience.") The inevitable consequences of his sin meant that his wife (the third one) was forced to leave him after much anguish and many attempts to rehabilitate him. It was also becoming increasingly more difficult for him to secure employment. He had no one's trust, not even his parents. The difficulties he faced because of this lack of trust resulted from dragging his foot against the universe, from violating certain of God's laws. He was lonely; he had lost the comfort of continuing companionship, and he had difficulty in finding employment. Most of the jobs he could get were poor ones that he disliked. But feel guilty? No!

Many Christians assume that everyone will feel as guilty as they do if they violate some particular standards. That is not true. Nor is the opposite, that if I don't feel guilty for something neither should you. We all tend to be a bit ethnocentric, culture-centered, or self-centered in this regard. We assume that everyone else's conscience should be or is like ours or that human conscience is hooked up as a direct pipeline from God. As I suggested in a previous chapter, it's the responsibility of every Christian to examine his conscience and to see that it meets the standards God sets. The command, "be not conformed to this world" applies particularly to our consciences. They need to be redeemed and sanctified the same as every other part of our being.

Values in Therapy

The fact that we may not feel guilty even though we have violated a law or standard of God has implications for treatment. Should the Christian therapist somehow get this person to feel guilty or work to change his values to fit more closely to God's values? If the reason for which this person has sought my services relates to values, I have a *responsibility* to make this a topic for consideration. I may tell him what I think will happen to him if he acts in such and such a way, that these are my beliefs, even though they aren't his. However, if there is no relationship between his reason for coming and his values, I may violate his personhood by forcing the issue. He has a right to choose his own values, however bad I think they are. God doesn't force the issue. Neither should I.

It is also true that Christians don't always agree what God's standards are in all areas. There are many gray areas where God has not spoken definitively and where we must arrive at our own construction of what is right for us. Here, too, we must not impose our constructions on others; share maybe, but not impose. While we acknowledge that values are a part of therapy, it is also true that the systematic and deliberate espousal of values is not the function of the therapist. He may do so as a person if asked, but not for a fee. As you can see, there are many ethical issues here. Unfortunately, many who call themselves Christian therapists seem to lack awareness of the ethical violations of using the therapy couch for a pulpit. That's the pharisee business again— covering sinful behavior in overtly righteous garb.

I am just as offended, however, by the many secular therapists who impose their values on clients. They do this by spoofing the individual's values by telling him it is wrong (a value) to feel guilty for something by encouraging behavior which deviates from that person's values, or by directly arguing for a reduction or change in values. They, too, have stepped out of the therapist role and have explicitly or implicitly declared their own values as the norm against which the client is to judge his. How pompous can you get? I'm not saying that the evaluation and clarification of values can't take place in therapy. Values need to be explicit to know what effect they may be having on a person.

This shows how important it is for anyone who works with people to be highly aware of his own values and not use the therapy room as a place to play God. Professionals in the mental health field are frequently offended by ministers who try to play therapist. But they will often play minister or philosopher without any qualms at all. The place for the espousal of values and the argument thereof is in the marketplace, not the therapy room.

If Your Conscience Hurts, Deal With It

What does all this say to the depressed person? It says that if you have the slightest inkling that you are not living up to your own values or standards that you believe are God-given, then you'd better come to grips with that in a therapeutic relationship or you'll likely not get the release for which you seek. And if the therapist ignores it, you'd be wise to find one who will make values a topic of consideration.

Don't Tranquilize Your Guilt Away

Amazingly, many people think that real guilt can be tranquilized away rather than faced and dealt with. Unfortunately pill pushing for emotional distress has become such an integral part of medicine, that it is routine in our society to try to deal with sin by chemical means. Time and again I see people who have violated their values develop some symptoms of tension and stress. They seek out their physician for these physical symptoms and receive whatever diagnostic tests seem appropriate. If the findings are negative the doctor will ask the patient if something is bothering him. A value problem, however, will seldom come out in response to such a direct question. Patients usually deny any stress or they throw out a decoy, a lesser stress in their life. (Pressure at work, finances, etc.) The doctor then prescribes valium or librium or an anti-depressant and sends them

160

on their way without getting to the root.

Now I realize that doctors usually don't have either the time or the tools to get at this dimension of stress and depression. Somehow, however, we need to do more than to dispense chemical conscience-relievers that only ultimately compound the problem of real guilt.

Respiratory Problems or Sin?

I can cite many examples. Take Dale, married more than eighteen years with two teenage children. His physician referred him to me. On three occasions at work Dale had found himself gasping for air, unable to catch his breath. The last time this had forced him to leave work. He had other symptoms as well, so his doctor put him in the hospital for tests. He was there for most of a week, but the tests showed nothing. They consulted a pulmonary specialist, but he found nothing. Fortunately, Dale's doctor didn't just call it nerves and tranquilize it away. Instead, the doctor sent Dale over to have him evaluated for whatever psychological causes might be contributing.

For the first time in many tense and anxious years Dale had an opportunity to face the issue. For ten years he had been involved homosexually with the same person. Again and again he had tried to call it off, only to compulsively return. On at least two occasions he had found himself driving madly down the road intending to end it all, but he was always held back by feelings of affection and responsibility to his wife and children. He became increasingly overwhelmed with guilt for the way he treated his wife. Evening after evening he had left her with the kids with the excuse of having to work. Then he would complain of being so tired that she couldn't expect him to be interested in sex. Nor could he go on vacations

161

with the family. He had tried, but always had to cut out early to get back to his "lover." The massive deceit and a great deal of self-revulsion had caught up with him.

To have tranquilized away his guilt would have perpetrated the destruction of this family and heightened the suicidal potential of this man. Luckily he had a doctor who didn't leave the patient with the stress unresolved or merely mitigated temporarily by drugs.

Nerves or Sin?

Lou Ellen is another example of this problem. She was a single working woman who lived with her invalid mother and father. Lou Ellen was raised in a Mennonite background and was moderately active in a Mennonite church. When I saw her she was a bundle of nerves and had been for a number of years. Two times she had been hospitalized in a psychiatric ward in a local hospital, and the second time she had received electric shock treatments. She had taken tranquilizers and anti-depressant medications of one kind or another for almost six years. Whenever the tension mounted or depression overtook her, she simply increased her pill intake. At times she was so drugged she was a virtual zombie. The medicine had side effects she didn't like, but it was better than the anxiety and depression.

It certainly wouldn't have occurred to anyone that sin was the problem facing Lou Ellen. She appeared pious, even super-cautious. Eventually Lou Ellen shared with me a problem she had been hiding for a long time. It was hard for her to tell me, and it didn't come out all at once but in bits and pieces. At first she told me about a time way back when she had taken a very small and insignificant object from the J. C. Penney store. She didn't tell me what—just that it wasn't worth much. In following sessions she told of many more episodes of stealing and constantly reassured me that it was never anything big. As we gently pursued, I learned that Lou Ellen had been a compulsive stealer for a long time. Her father had become suspicious. In her room he saw so many things that she never mentioned buying. When he questioned her, she got mad. He was old and confused and embarrassed and didn't know what to do.

Lou Ellen had become trapped by her own sinful behavior. The more she stole the more condemned she felt. The more condemned she felt, the more anxious and depressed she became. She was anxious that she might be caught, anxious because she thought her father knew, and miserable and depressed because she felt driven to do it again and again. The pills could not remove the guilt Lou Ellen felt. With her value system she simply couldn't approve of stealing. When she would steal she couldn't sleep. When she couldn't sleep she would take more pills. When she didn't take the pills she'd get anxious, scared, and depressed. With her precious pills she could at least live with herself most of the time, however uncomfortably.

Interestingly enough when that Pandora's box opened, all kinds of things started to fit together. Lou Ellen had harbored longstanding anger at her parents for their stiff and rigid ways. She was angry at them for trapping her into remaining at home to help her invalid mother. She was angry at her married brothers and sisters for having left her with all the responsibility and grief. She was angry for never having felt free to leave home. She was angry at the whole world for the trap her life had become and angry at God for letting it all happen this way. But she could never express to any of these people the anger that had accumulated in her soul.

Once Lou Ellen had come clean with herself and

163

others about these problems and had made what restitution was possible, she was a new person—free of her need to steal, free of the anger that had complicated her life beyond measure, and free of all those pills.

Depression—God's Intent?

Maybe, just maybe, some anxiety and depression are God's way of saying we can't drag our feet against the universe without emotional wear and tear. Perhaps in the economy of God, the misery that accompanies guilt and bad behavior is all quite functional. These miserable feelings make us pay attention to our waywardness and deal with it. The depression and agony stem from the dissonance between our values and our behavior. Maybe these are gifts of God.

If this is true, then to try to subdue or eradicate these feelings through drugs may actually be counterproductive over the long term. In the short run they seem helpful because they dull our minds to misery. But they prevent us from facing up to the causes of our misery, and they allow our emotional distress to perpetrate itself indefinitely.

Now don't hear me saying that all medications for emotional disorder are bad. No, there are situations and disorders where the use of such drugs is appropriate and necessary. I question their use where one has violated his values and is hiding that fact from himself and others.

In our present society, however, we routinely administer drugs without precluding this possibility. Doctors don't have the time and frequently don't have the tools to enable them to differentiate this functional distress from the more malignant types. I object to the promiscuous use of these medications, not necessarily to the medications themselves. We have come to the point in our soci-

164

ety where drug abuse by prescription far exceeds the abuse of drugs by street abusers. When we interfere with God's intention of functional emotional distress, I am convinced that we will do so only at our own individual and collective peril.

This is not to say that people will read the signals of such functional emotional distress accurately, nor that they will necessarily pay heed to the signals and mend their ways and repair their souls. They must choose. They have the God-given right to ignore the dissonance in their lives and to tranquilize it away if they can. But do we need to prescribe it for them?

David and Saul

I think that David is a biblical example of depression which is the result of sin. Remember his affair with Bathsheba? Deceit and foul play by David followed the act. David ordered the placement of Bathsheba's husband, Uriah, into a battle situation where he would almost surely meet death.

Imagine the guilt that must have overwhelmed David. He had been caught in a complicated web of bad behavior. To cover up the fact that he had gotten Bathsheba pregnant, he called Uriah back from battle, thinking that Uriah would have sexual relations with his wife and thus get David out of trouble. But Uriah, being loyal to some soldier protocol of the time, did not sleep in his home but with his soldiers. David then tried to get Uriah drunk, but to no avail, so he then had Uriah sent to the hottest forefront of the battle. As it so often happens with our bad behavior, one thing led to another. Some believe that David wrote Psalm 32 following these despicable events. Note his depression, and note also the way out of this depression.

Blessed is he whose transgression is forgiven,
whose sin is covered.

Blessed is the man to whom the Lord
imputes no iniquity,
and in whose spirit there is no deceit.

When I declared not my sin, my body wasted
away (loss of weight?) through my
groaning all day long.

For day and night thy hand was
heavy upon me; (no relief, day or night)

My strength was dried up as by the
heat of summer (fatigue and exhaustion).

I acknowledge my sin to thee,
and I did not hide my iniquity;

I said, "I will confess my transgressions
to the Lord,"

Then Thou didst forgive the guilt of
my sin.

Here we have the symptoms of depression as well as an acknowledgement by the writer that these symptoms were the result of sin. Then he got relief by facing it squarely, confessing his wrongdoing, and accepting God's forgiveness. No pills, no shock treatments, no therapy.

What if he could have successfully tranquilized this guilt and depression away? He might not have dealt with it, and he might have remained in a state of anxious depression, worrisome guilt, and dulled senses.

Saul is another biblical example, but with a less happier ending. He, too, had severe depression. At such times music provided a kind of release from his anguish, so he called David to play the lyre for him. Many depressed people say that immersing themselves in music provides some momentary escape for them, especially when they are alone. When we're alone, of course, we have to deal with ourselves, our bad behavior, and attendant misery, and that's difficult if you're caught up in some sinful behavior. To immerse yourself in music, simply gets your mind off the problem temporarily. Music did lift Saul's spirits, but it meant that he didn't face himself, so the depressions came back. Saul had broken certain commandments of God, and Samuel had tried, unsuccessfully, to get Saul to deal with this.

Brutalization of Spouse

When we violate our own standards of behavior, depression often results. And in such depressions we may, as a defense mechanism, rationalize our bad feelings and problems and blame them on someone else. I have frequently seen this lead to the systematic brutalization of an innocent bystander.

Mr. Voytek and his wife came to me for marriage counseling. He had a thousand complaints about her which he seemed almost compelled to enumerate and in great detail. He avoided no opportunity to put her down and make her look bad, and his comments were cruel and merciless.

He couldn't stand to have sex with her because of her body odor. She didn't keep up her appearance; she was "sloppy fat, looks like a pig half the time." Nothing about her attracted him. He didn't know why he had married her. She couldn't keep the house up. She never had been a decent sex partner; she just "lay there like a cold fish." What husband could go on living like that? And she had

167

no respect for money, never had. He had to slave away, sometimes at two jobs, just to pay off her bills for heaven knows what. Some of the things he said about her and in front of her we can't print. The only thing good about her that he could suggest was that she wasn't a half-bad mother to the children.

She, of course, was reduced to tears and confusion. Most of these complaints she had never heard at all in the first ten years of their marriage. In the last eight months, however, this barrage of complaint and dissatisfaction came forth, and he cruelly put her down at home. As soon as he entered the house, he would begin a tirade of complaints and sarcastic remarks. She couldn't do *anything* right.

It was quite obvious that he was in a state of agitated depression. He couldn't eat or sleep, and lost twenty-four pounds in four months. He couldn't sit down for even a minute without having to get up and pace around or leave the house. He came home only to leave the house in a huff, yet he was exhausted and fatigued all the time. His mood was sullen and blue. At one time he had engaged in happy horseplay with the kids when he had come home from work. Now he was only irritated with them. They incurred his wrath for breathing, and several times he had totally lost control of himself with them. One time when his son's bicycle was in the way, he pushed it up against the wall of the garage with the car.

Marriage counseling didn't work out. Mr. Voytek was in no way ready to remedy anything. He simply used these many complaints of his wife to justify his need to get out of the marriage, which he did. Soon, however, the real story surfaced. About ten months before that Mr. Voytek, an appliance repair man, had found a young, recently divorced gal crying on his shoulder while he was repairing her refrigerator. They had gotten involved almost immediately, and he had seen her every day since that first one. They planned on marriage almost from the beginning, but he had to get out of his first marriage. That was his problem. Unfortunately, he chose to reduce his wife to nothing in his own eyes to accomplish his desires and thus avoid guilt.

When I saw this man a number of months later, he was in bad shape. His new relationship was not working out, and he was having some second thoughts about how much he had bad-mouthed his ex-wife. He could see what purpose this had served for him, and he was in a state of wretched misery.

Kit had a similar problem. She came for help alone, but complained all about her husband and how wretched her life was because of him. He didn't do anything right. He didn't know how to make love. He didn't show affection very much. He didn't earn a decent living. He wasn't outgoing enough. He wasn't a very good father. He didn't keep up his appearance. He was overweight (about ten to fifteen pounds). He didn't respect her mother and would just read when they would visit her. He had no goals. His table manners left much to be desired. On and on it went.

I was startled to see what kind of fellow Jack was when he finally came in. (She resisted somewhat having him included in the discussions.) He just didn't match her descriptions, in fact, appeared almost opposite in many ways. He was quite confused by her behavior. He could see how depressed she was and tried his best to help. But the more he tried to help, the more infuriated with him and depressed she became.

Like Mrs. Voytek, he had not heard these complaints for the first nine years of marriage. For the last year, however, the antagonism between them increased. It was almost as if she wanted to find fault or went looking for things to complain about. At times it appeared she intended to provoke him, as though she wanted him to act badly, to lose his cool. She couldn't stand to have him pay any attention to her or try to be affectionate, in spite of her earlier complaints that he had been lax and never touched her.

When the story eventually came out, Jack was furious, furious with her for her unfaithfulness and furious with himself for having tried so hard to make things better. Most of all, he was furious for not having read the situation more clearly.

Not quite two years ago an outside speaker had come to their church for some special meetings and had stayed in their home. Kit and this speaker had a number of long discussions, and something clicked between them. She thought they both were aware of it but nothing happened then. Later he had called a couple of times when in the area and she had written a few times. Before long he stopped in during the day time when he had meetings in a community about 100 miles away. He would come over in the morning, then return to his meetings in the evening. This time they had gotten sexually involved. From then on she was frustrated at not being able to be with this new exciting lover. The more she wanted to be with her paramour, the less she was able to be nice at home. The affair had continued, but had all recently burst when she found out that she wasn't the only lover in this evangelist's life. That had come as a crushing blow. When she found that she was one of a crowd, her love turned to hatred and bitterness. Not only had she been taken, but she had spent over a year being absolutely nasty and provocative to a husband she knew loved and cared for her deeply if not always passionately. She was numb for awhile, but the depression eventually lifted as she started to put the pieces of her life back together.

Integrity Therapy

Before we leave this concept of depression as a result of sin, let me introduce you to a theory of psychopathology (the study of psychological disorder) which is based on this same idea. We call it Integrity Therapy, and the name most associated with its formulation is O. Hobart Mowrer, research professor of psychology at the University of Illinois.

Dr. Mowrer was a psychologist who had reached the highest point of his profession by being elected president of the American Psychological Association. He had made numerous technical contributions through his research in the area of learning and became famous in his field. Early in his career, Dr. Mowrer had been very interested and committed to the psychoanalytic or Freudian school of thought. However, through his own first-hand experience with depression, he came to repudiate that position.

Dr. Mowrer knew very well that the cause of his depression was misbehavior on his part, not some obscure childhood problems as the Freudian theory claimed. If you are interested in Mowrer's own personal experiences of depression and in how he arrived at this theory, you can find it in his book, *Abnormal Reactions or Actions.*

Mowrer considers his theory to be almost the opposite of Freud's in terms of how he views guilt. Freud considered guilt an unfortunate hangover from overly strict parents. A quote from Freud shows this. "The disease of the neurotic is his guilt. This guilt is, in itself, an evil and its removal is good." Mowrer felt that therapists of this persuasion tended to encourage people to violate their consciences and to reassure patients that they need not feel guilty. He suggests that for Freudians all guilt is

171

merely guilt feelings and should be ignored or removed. It also has the result, Mowrer suggests, of making people not feel responsible for whatever emotional problems or symptoms they were having. They could blame their bad behavior or sick behavior on their parents or others. They could say that their bad behavior was the product of warped or unfortunate emotions over which they did not have control. The basic problem according to Freudians, lay in the emotional life of the patient, not his behavior.

Mowrer reverses this thinking. He says that emotional disturbance is the result of abnormal behavior, not the other way around. An individual, he says, becomes fearful and guilt-ridden *because* of his behavior and then develops symptoms which reflect this inner *dis-ease.* He sums this idea up by saying "that in psychopathology the primary basic cause is deliberate, choice-mediated behavior of a socially disapproved nature which results in emotional disturbance and insecurity." And in Mowrer's view they *ought* to disturb the individual so as to get him to come clean with his misbehavior whatever that may be.

Mowrer says that the Freudian view completely reverses Mosaic morality. "Health, pleasure, and virtue will come not from observance of the Mosaic law, but by its disregard." (I might say, if you are not already aware of it, that the Freudian view has historically been the most influential and dominant view of emotional and mental problems.)

Two additional quotes from Mowrer portray his position quite vividly. " . . . the so-called psychoneurosis and functional psychosis can be understood only in terms of palpable misconduct which has been neither confessed nor expiated." And " . . . that we fall ill, emotionally, not because of deprivation, but depravity." So Mowrer, it appears, believes that *all* emotional disorder that is not the result of some direct brain damage, injury, or impairment is the product of misbehavior. That almost sounds like a fundamentalist Bible-pounding preacher talking, but Mowrer is not even speaking from a theological or religious framework. This is a straight, secular view of how people get emotionally disturbed and depressed. Also, don't forget, this is the view of a man who, himself, suffered severe depression.

Mowrer says there are two basic steps to emotional problems. One is to *choose* to do socially forbidden things, and the second is to try to hide or deny that we have done them. It is this combination of misbehavior and hiding it that he feels is so deadly in terms of mental problems. He says the sickness is not in what the person is *feeling* but in what he is *doing*.

Mowrer refers to the story of Adam and Eve as the model of emotional problems. Adam sins and then he tries to hide. As a result of his concealment, he feels guilt and loss of peace of mind. Had Adam, Mowrer suggests, gone to the Lord after violating the rules, the outcome may have been different. We can say the same, I believe, about Mr. Voytek, Lou Ellen, and Kit. Had they, once they had violated their consciences, come clean with themselves, they would not have had to suffer the depression that they eventually experienced. Nor could the rationalization and justification defense mechanisms work. Adam tried to pass the buck to Eve. "The woman whom Thou gavest to me, she gave me of the tree and I did eat." This sounds like Kit and Mr. Voytek who tried to pass the buck for their own distress on to their spouses.

Not All Depression Is the Result of Sin

I want to sound one note of caution before I finish this chapter. We must be careful that we do not insist that all

173

depression is a result of sin. I depart from Mowrer if he means (and I think he does) that *all* emotional disorders except those due to brain injury, disease, or impairment, are the result of sin and the consequent hiding of that behavior. As this chapter well indicates, I am convinced that a great deal of depression is the product of sin. However, I am also equally convinced that *not all* depression is the product of sin. There are numerous reasons why people get depressed. Sin is one of them, maybe even a dominant one, but not the only one. In fact, one other major cause of depression I have found is that which I would say is due to sin in the life of another. I referred to this briefly in chapter one in speaking of persons whose mates have been unfaithful to them. In that case it is not their sin, but their spouse's sin which has resulted in their depression. The bad behavior of parents may result in depression in their children.

Yet another note of caution is in order. Believing that someone is depressed because they have been misbehaving, should make us no less sympathetic and concerned about them. They need help just as much as any other depressed person. They need help to break that connection between their symptoms and the hiding.

No sinner (as a Christian I believe all men have this problem and that includes me) has the right to view another sinner as something contemptible or beneath him. Nothing in Christianity warrants that. That, in fact, is just that miserable old Pharisee wrapped up in Christian garb. Shun it as vigorously as you would depression.

174

CHAPTER X

CONFESSION IS GOOD FOR THE SOUL

DALE WAS A graduate student in a university chemistry department and had been doing outstandingly well. His advisors and professors had given him a lot of privileges and personal attention, and he had become increasingly confident that his Ph.D. was in the bag. Suddenly, however, not long before his comprehensive exams, the bottom seemed to drop out on him.

He couldn't study; he couldn't get himself to concentrate. The comprehensive exams meant that he needed to have a comprehensive, overall knowledge of his field, because in those exams he could be asked questions on any aspect of that field. So now, more than ever, he needed to read and retain vast amounts of material. But right now there was no way he could sit down and read, much less concentrate and retain anything. He couldn't even stay with the newspaper for more than five minutes.

He had other symptoms as well. He had lost a lot of weight in the last four or five months. Since he had been quite heavy, he actually welcomed this, except for the expense for new clothes. He just had no appetite, he reported. His wife couldn't believe it, for he had appeared hungry *all* the time during eight years of marriage. Donna felt this was all anxiety about the upcoming comprehensive exams, so she wasn't especially troubled about it.

A number of times, however, perhaps five times or so, he had had problems catching his breath. Now *that* she was concerned about, but Dale assured her that this, too, was just nerves related to the exam threat. She wanted him to see a doctor about that, but he dismissed it. It had been rather traumatic for her though, because it had always occurred either when they were in bed or in the middle of some conversation. It was like an attack of some kind, and you couldn't know ahead of time that it was coming. He'd just choke and gasp and have to get up and go out. Then he would soon be all right; but it was still scary.

As a graduate assistant Dale had responsibility for a couple of college freshman courses. Here, too, he had problems. It was important that he do well, as this, too, was an area on which he was evaluated, but he couldn't keep his mind on the subject matter. Several times when he'd been lecturing to the class, he had completely blacked out and couldn't remember what he had just said or where he was in a sequence of thoughts. This was not only embarrassing but somewhat alarming. He had broken out in a sweat at those moments. It shook him so that he told the students he felt sick and let them go.

This development baffled his professors. He had failed to hand in two papers and had just about dropped out of a research project in which he had a major responsibility. He had gone to his advisor and told him what was happening and how depressed and blue he was and that he had no energy and was just totally unable to study. They suggested he get professional help.

When he came to me, he didn't have the vaguest idea, he said, why he was so depressed. He had never experienced anything like this before. He came to see if I could get him out of these depressed feelings so that he could study for his comprehensives with the same efficiency and energy he had shown before. He wasn't sleeping and was totally exhausted. Yet, though he was not sleeping well, he just couldn't get up in the morning either. That was the hardest part of all, in fact. He just couldn't face the day, and yet he knew he had all this work to prepare for comprehensives. Could I get him back on track?

It seemed a rather straightforward problem at first glance. I remembered how anxious I had been before comprehensives. It was probably one of the most tense times I had ever had, and I had a lot of physical symptoms from that tension. I knew that frequently this was true for many others toward the end of a doctoral program. You put in maybe three, four years of study, courses, and research, yet if you fail the comprehensives, you have nothing to show for all the years of effort. So the pressure is really on. It seemed that Dale's depression was just a product of the fear of failure and all the anxious anticipation that was going on in his head as he got closer to this critical juncture in his career. All the anxiety and hard work had exhausted him, leaving him depressed.

I suggested a complete physical first of all. Dale resisted as he felt the symptoms were just all tension stuff, but I made it a requirement before I would counsel further. The doctor told him what he expected, but we needed to make sure—there was nothing physically wrong, it was just tension and nerves.

Next we began to work on whatever head stuff was going on that was getting him so upset. The more we talked the more I heard a thousand complaints about Donna. Before long he was saying maybe he needed to get out of this marriage. At that point I brought Donna into the counseling. The last four months or so had been a difficult time in their relationship. She felt he had been constantly irritable and critical, but then she figured this

177

was all due to anxiety over the comprehensives, so she had tried to ignore it. The more she ignored it, however, the more angry and irritable he had become. This was all so unlike Dale, she said. It was as if he'd had a total change of personality over these last six months; but that, too, she attributed to the upcoming comprehensives.

It was now getting so bad Dale felt he had to leave the house. Maybe he should live somewhere else until exams were over. But that made little sense. Financially they could not afford the luxury of two apartments. Instead she offered to stay out of his way as much as possible, but that didn't seem to improve anything. He couldn't stand her presence, however little it seemed.

Why all of a sudden all this marital unhappiness and irritation at Donna? I could see nothing building up to this in their marriage. It appeared to happen all at once, or so it had seemed to Donna. Dale denied that, saying that he'd been unhappy almost from the very beginning of the marriage. But then why hadn't he said anything, why had he seemed so happy with her and the marriage before?

Before long some unexplained events and situations—money, time, over concern for appearance, etc.—came out in our discussions. Dale became enraged, even mean and vicious with Donna for bringing these up. It seemed as if he took every opportunity to hurt her feelings and to get her to feel badly about herself.

Dale denied anything other than the anxiety over exams and unhappiness with Donna that was troubling him. We got nowhere in counseling, neither with the depression nor clarification of the marital distress. He became increasingly agitated and irritable. Blowups occurred over nothing, and several times he implied suicidal feelings or threats to Donna.

Then it all blew open. Yes, there was someone else,

another graduate student in the program. They had worked on some research together, a computer program. Then he started going over to her apartment during the day a lot, and before long they'd gotten sexually involved. This hadn't bothered the girl apparently. She didn't think there was anything wrong with it or the fact he was married, so he thought it was okay. If this girl were being hurt by it or expecting more, then it would have been wrong, he reasoned with himself. Increasingly, however, Dale found himself more and more tense, upset, and irritable. He was violating his own values and knew it. He knew that his contract with Donna did not include this kind of behavior.

When it came out, it was almost as if a huge burden were taken off his back. There was a great deal of grief and anguish, but the heavy depression lifted. When he finally owned up to his behavior, came out of hiding and quit the deceitful pretense with Donna, he could face the day again.

On two occasions he had tried to break off this relationship, once for almost five weeks, but the tension had only mounted for him, even become deeper. At that time he had felt that if his problems were in any way related to this affair, he should have gotten relief, but he didn't. Now he wondered why that had been? And why the relief now if not before when he had stopped seeing her?

Coming Clean

I have seen this story repeated many times—depression and agitation getting worse and worse, acute irritation with one's spouse or others, culminating in inability to function on the job or elsewhere. Often I see the signs of addiction, of someone compulsively hooked on something from which he cannot disentangle himself.

Then when he comes clean with himself and others, the depression lifts, the agitation ceases, and the addictive characteristics cease. These people have violated their own values by failing to live up to them in some way. This produces guilt, that cutting edge of conscience that is called into action by the dissonance that exists between one's behavior and one's values. This guilt then forces the person into hiding his behavior from the people with whom he is intimately involved and the group of people from whom he has derived his identity. It may also involve hiding from himself. I have seen people simply deny any wrongdoing through exceedingly devious and irrational logic. They have set about to deceive not only others, but also themselves. They align their behavior with their values by irrational arguments directed against themselves. This is their way of trying to hide from themselves.

I remember one married couple, Larry and Suzanne, who came in to see me in a high state of agitation. Larry carried a large Bible with him and identified himself as a very active member of a conservative, fundamentalist church. He immediately faced me with a series of doctrinal questions to test my Christian values and commitment. Did I believe in the authority of Scripture, the substitutionary atonement of Christ, and so on? For a few moments I thought I had to take ordination vows for his church before we could counsel. I knew the nature of his concerns, however, so I cooperated.

Once that was past, he launched into a whole scale attack to convince his wife and me that his desire to get out of his marriage in no way contradicted the Scripture as he understood it. Divorce did not violate his values, he claimed, and he had a whole series of biblical references to justify his view. The logic lacked a lot, however. He indicated that their marriage had never been right from the beginning. It had begun falsely and immorally, so it was really not a marriage in God's sight. In their courtship, because he was aware of the lack of strictness in her background and "solid Christian principles in her home," he had been "concerned with her chastity" and had "tested her, but it failed and we had sex before marriage." Then he felt morally obligated to marry her. For the next nine years, he said he was tormented with thoughts that she might have had sex with others before marriage. "I don't love her; I never did; and I never can," he said. This is the first time in nine years of marriage, however, that this had come out. He had always expressed his love freely, Suzanne thought, and only recently had it come to a halt.

In later sessions it came out that there was a woman at work, a "really genuine Christian" whom he had "admired" now for two or three years. He had even laid awake nights thinking of what a wonderful Christian woman she was, he reported, but "not immoral thoughts in any way" he assured me (or should I say assured himself). On impulse he had called this woman one evening and told her of his admiration. Just like that!

During this time his wife reported he was agitated and antagonistic and complained endlessly of how she handled the children and kept the house. He also criticized her failure to work more in the church. He informed me he had read the New Testament thoroughly in the last two and a half weeks to see "if in any way he could be in error," and God had showed him that he should get divorced. The marriage had been immorally conceived, and was therefore, an adulterous union. He regretted that he hadn't seen this sooner. "All this," he summarized, "has given me a deeper love of Christ."

This massive onslaught of argument and denial was the only way he could continue in the direction he was

181

going without being overwhelmed with guilt. He was trying to convince his own conscience that there was no discrepancy between his values and his behavior or intentions.

Thankfully I had met up with this kind of massive denial before and knew better than to get trapped in the theoretical argument. In our following sessions we merely reflected back to him his own contradictions in his thinking. Finally the dissonance was too apparent, even to him. As he talked he had to reach further and further for justification of his thoughts and intentions. Finally, they became so ludicrous, he could no longer deny the obvious. When he faced himself he was amazed at how devious, irrational, and illogical he had become in trying to live with his hurting conscience.

We see then that this hiding can take place in a number of devious and deceptive ways. But however it occurs, it becomes an extremely heavy load that drags a person down deeper and deeper into agitation and depression. I have seen many people attempt to cope with these feelings by excessive drinking or excessive business, only to compound the problem. But, no matter how the hiding takes place, the cure is the same—openness with oneself and with significant others.

"Confession is good for the soul" is an ancient maxim. Psychology has nothing new here except, perhaps, some deeper understandings of some of the dynamics of confession. We've known from time immemorial that confession can provide relief for inner turmoil and anguish. We see many references in great literature to this dynamic in man's thought and behavior. Shakespeare's *Macbeth* is a good example. The need for confession, the disastrous effects of hiding, and the release provided by confession has been documented in the great literature of every age.

The word "confession" will offend some since it has moralistic overtones. Therefore, they use labels such as "self-disclosure," or "self-revelation," or "ventilation." I don't care what you call it, the principles remain.

The Bible makes no bones about this principle. It permeates both Old and New Testaments. In I John 1:8 we read, "If we say we have no sin, we deceive ourselves, [remember Larry] and the truth is not in us. If we confess our sins, he is faithful and just, and will forgive our sins and cleanse us from all unrighteousness." Here we have it. We must first of all quit deceiving ourselves, quit pretending that sin is not our problem. We need to let it all hang out, to confess our sin, to admit to ourselves the truth about ourselves and then, and only then, will cleansing take place. I like that word cleansing. Have you ever been all sweaty, greasy, and dirty and felt the relief that comes from taking a good shower? That's just like the psychological relief that comes from confession. We rid ourselves of the dirt that clings and clogs up the pores of our soul.

Or how about the biblical command to "confess your sins to one another, that you may be healed" (Jas. 5:16)? Can it be more straightforward than that? Here is the way toward healing and restoration, a way out of the darkness and the tumult of depression that results from real guilt. It is simple, really, not complicated, but very difficult. It is one thing to believe it and another thing to do it. If you've been there you know exactly what I mean. That step is a very difficult one to take. Many find it impossible.

Confession is very much a part of psychotherapy, whether admitted by therapists or not. Call it what he may, the dynamics of confession are clearly a part of all psychotherapy systems, worked right into the warp and woof of technique and procedure. Like the medical doctor who only makes it possible for the healing processes to come into play, but himself does not do the healing, just so with the psychotherapist. He can aid in bringing about the opportunity for confession but the cleansing effects are not his doing at all. Like the doctor who may allow the mending of broken bones to take place by setting them together, or the healing of a wound by cleaning out the dirt and infection, the psychotherapist merely sets the scene so that healing has a chance.

Go back and read Psalms 32 and 51. Notice how much confession is a part of those psalms. Notice, too, the relief which follows confession there and in these excerpts from Psalm 51:

> Wash me thoroughly from my iniquity,
>   and cleanse me from my sin!
> For I know my transgressions,
>   and my sin is ever before me.
>
> Behold, thou desirest truly in the inward being,
>   therefore teach me wisdom in my secret heart.
> Purge me with hyssop, and I shall be clean,
>   wash me, and I shall be whiter than snow.
> Fill me with joy and gladness; let the
>   bones which thou hast broken rejoice.
>
> Restore to me the joy of thy salvation,
>   and uphold me with a willing spirit.

And in Psalm 32 after those vivid descriptions of the agonies of depression, notice the way out—and the outcome of depression:

> I acknowledge my sin to thee, and
>   I did not hide my iniquity.

184

I said, "I will confess my transgressions
    unto the Lord";
then thou didst forgive the guilt of
    my sin.

Then at the end:

Be glad in the Lord, and rejoice, O righeous,
    and shout for joy, all you upright in heart.

The Benefits of Confession

Let's take a look at some of the many benefits of confession. As we have just implied, confession has a cleansing function. Like the removal of dirt from a wound, it opens the way for healing. Or like the lancing of a boil, it allows for the removal of infectious matter so that healing can begin. Confession is not the healing itself, rather it is the cleansing that allows the healing forces to begin their work. For example, in marriages like Dale and Donna's or Larry and Suzanne's, there is little we can do to repair the relationship until the infectious material has been cleansed away. Attempts to restructure the lives of depressed persons will come to naught until they tend to the guilt which causes the depression.

This cleansing role is vividly described in Shakespeare's *Macbeth:*

Canst thou not minister to a mind diseased,
Pluck from the memory a rooted sorrow,
Raze out the written troubles of the brain,
And with sweet oblivious antidote
Cleanse the stuffed bosom of the perilous stuff
    which weighs against the heart.

185

>Give sorrow words; the grief that does not
>speak whispers the o'er fraught
>heart and bids it break.

A famous psychologist, William James, speaking of the need for confession, uses the phrase to "exteriorize our rottenness." Like the rotten apple in a bushel, we must remove it or else the rottenness will spread to others. Just so with the need for confession. If we fail to exteriorize our rottenness, we leave ourselves open to the spreading of the infection throughout the entire system. I have seen people whose physical and mental health have rapidly deteriorated for failure to do this. They have developed a whole host of physical problems, usually tension-produced problems throughout their bodies, or severe emotional and mental problems compounded by depression or anxiety. I have frequently seen paranoid delusions (totally unwarranted suspicions) emerge from the uncleansed conscience of persons so distressed. Interestingly, this can often result in suspiciousness and accusation of others of the very behavior of which they themselves have been guilty. Or even psychotic symptoms (where loss of reality contact occurs; what most people think of as "crazy").

O. H. Mowrer says in his book *The New Group Therapy* (a collection of essays on the need for confession and openness), "Most of us live depleted existences: weak, zestless, apprehensive, pessimistic, neurotic. The reason is that when we perform a good deed, we advertise it and thus collect and enjoy the credit then and there. When we do something cheap and mean, however, we carefully hide and deny it (if we can) with the result that the credit for our acts of this kind remains with us and accumulates." Thus confession can stop the spread of infection from going further in both our physical and emotional systems.

Confession or self-disclosure also reestablishes communication between man and God and between man and man. I have become very interested in how guilt jams communications, especially in marital relationships. Frequently I'll find that the so-called guilty party just can't stand to talk to his or her spouse. Discussions about the relationship problem get absolutely nowhere. Actually the wayward spouses will go to great lengths to avoid discussion. Confession removes the barrier that makes communication so difficult, if not impossible.

It follows that confession ends the withdrawal and loneliness that accompanies the hiding. Pretense and deceit are no longer necessary. So often I have heard how someone who is caught up in this sort of bad behavior will shun all the people they previously identified as friends. At first they don't want to go to some event or be with some friends who had previously been a fixed part of their lives. The other spouse is baffled. This is something new. Then it extends to many others. The old friends "don't stimulate" anymore. They want new ones. What's happening, of course, is that they don't want to have to face the old crowd. That reminds them that they are in hiding and feel guilty. New friends don't have expectations they may not be living up to. They will also choose new friends who don't hold to the same values as the old crowd, particularly in the area of the violation. Confession removes all this need to avoid former friends.

Determining Responsibility

Confession also allows us to recognize personal responsibility, or at least it makes possible a means of determining responsibility. So often in cases involving the violation of values, the guilty party has gone through a long sequence of self-justification that attributes the blame and responsibility to others. "I'm irritable because of my unruly children," or "your mother's on my back." "I'm depressed because of the bills," or "the boss requires too much of me at work."

Many times I've seen the innocent party accept these justifications. I remember one husband who attributed his bad mood, irritability, and depression to the long hours he had to work. Actually he was working less than he ever had in his life, but he was making daily trips out of town to visit his lover. When his wife bought his story, it made him feel more guilty and in time more irritable and depressed. I remember another who attributed his depression and agitation to financial pressures. His wife believed him, but the real pressure came from a gambling addiction. When she sympathized with him and even made moves to get a job (which he knew she did not want to do), he felt even greater guilt, and the vicious circle became more entrenched in his life.

Clarification

Another benefit of confession is that it allows for clarification of the problem. Emotional problems are often highly complicated, and as a marriage counselor I try to avoid the trap of trying to find out where a certain problem got started. When one says I did such and such because you did thus and so, the other responds that he did that specific thing because of some thing the other spouse said or did. And they in turn because of something the other had done, and back and forth it goes. Even if you find a beginning point for this sequence of blame, the supposedly initiating party will only say they said such and such because at some time about two months back the other had said thus and so. It's hopeless. You cannot assess blame in relationships.

188

To clarify the problem we need to define the nature of it. Without honest confession and self-disclosure, this is impossible. You end up working with ghosts, non-existent problems or pseudo-problems or decoys thrown out to distract you. I wonder how often couples leave marriage counseling or individuals leave therapy unhappy and dissatisfied with the results because someone avoided confession. I never cease to be amazed how much people are willing to pay those of us in the mental health field to help them with their bad feelings, yet play avoidance games with getting to the root of the matter. I guess they hope that the bad feelings can be removed without having to deal with the real causes.

It is also true that real guilt and false guilt are often mixed or even intertwined. I find this especially true in working with depressed people. Only honest confession can start to untangle these two.

The Igniting of Will Power

Probably the most significant benefit that follows confession is that it sets the torch to will power. Will power cannot be activated, it seems, without confession. Alcoholics struggle with their booze battles and get nowhere until they admit that they *are* alcoholic and need help. Only then can they begin to draw on that will power that has so completely eluded them.

It's obvious that loss of will power is a major component of depression. It is one of the tragic consequences of depression, for it leads to the vicious circle of not trying, withdrawing, and inwardness that in turn only makes the person more depressed. Most depressed persons cut themselves off from others. As they do so they also cut off the potential for renewed will power and the means to get themselves out of this misery.

189

Melanie was such a case. She claimed to be a Christian, came from a strict, devout home, and attended an evangelical church. She had been involved in a number of adulterous relationships, two times with other men in the church. She described these episodes by saying, "And I was supposed to be a Christian at the time." She felt, as she said, "a rotten person." She had been to the altar at her church many times feeling horribly guilty, but all to no avail. "I pray, pray, pray, and nothing happens," she said. She would resolve never to get involved again and beg for God's strength, but the feelings would build up, the desire to have another affair would overwhelm her, and the story would repeat itself. She also experienced an increasing loss of will power.

Will power is sociological. By that I mean that it is not really an individual matter, but a matter of involvement and identification with others. This in turn provides us with the support and strength we need to fight the battle against whatever it is we are hooked on or that has us in its power. The type of addiction makes no difference. Alcohol, food, money, gambling, other women, other men, praise from others, nice clothing, cars, work, drugs—the principle is the same. When we confess the problem to others they can help us with the struggle of staying straight.

Bonhoeffer (the renowned German theologian who was martyred in World War II for opposing Hitler), in his magnificent little book, *Life Together,* puts it this way: "In confession the break through to community takes place. Sin demands to have a man by himself. It withdraws him from the community. The more isolated a person is the more destructive will be the power of sin over him, and the more deeply he becomes involved in it, the more disastrous is his isolation. Sin wants to remain unknown . . . " (p. 112).

Look at some obvious will power problems such as losing weight and problem drinking. Why is it, do you suppose, that the group factor plays such a critical role in the ability to cope successfully with these problems? Because it's a matter of will power, and will power is derived from the identification with and support of others. By simply joining such groups one has confessed to having a problem. Weight Watchers, TOPS (Take Off Pounds Successfully), Over-Eaters Anonymous, Alcoholics Anonymous, Gamblers Anonymous—they all require an admission of the problem as a prerequisite. Alcoholics Anonymous requires a person to say again and again, "I am an alcoholic." Without such an admission (confession), there will be no will power. The person must admit he can't do it himself.

O. H. Mowrer advocates openness with others as the way out of *all* emotional problems. In his book, *The New Group Therapy,* he says, " . . . will power—that is, the capacity to make the right decisions and to *act* upon them—is a function of whether one is *in* or *out* of community. This means quite simply, that if we follow the policy of keeping our lives open to inspection, we find that our wills are suprisingly strong . . . if we adopt a policy of secrecy and deception, so that others *can't* watch us, then we have no resistance to temptation and our wills progressively deteriorate" (p. 61). Or even more comprehensively, "The crucial element in mental health is the degree of openness and communion which a person has *with his fellow men"* (p. iii). Or in his article entitled *Malconditioning or Misbehavior,* he says, "Thus one arrives at the view that there is no possibility of a successful *private* treatment of neurosis (either in a religious or secular context) for the reason that privacy, concealment, secrecy, and defensiveness is the essence of the difficulty."

191

Confess to Whom?

Protestant Christians will quickly ask if it isn't sufficient to confess to God. The whole fabric of Protestantism, based as it is on Reformation theology, is called into question here. Martin Luther in no uncertain terms proclaimed that man needs *no* mediator between himself and God but Jesus Christ. Luther was incensed with the practice of the Catholic Church at that time for requiring that a fee be paid for the privilege of confession to a priest and for the forgiveness that followed. Forgiveness was "on sale." Luther vehemently opposed such perversity and rightly so. But the danger is that we go too far the other way. We confess directly to God, and forgiveness is without price. We then fail to derive the value of open confession which cements us to a group of likewise erstwhile sinners, who mutually aid and abet one another in their need to resist continuing temptation.

The Bible is not vague here. It says, "Therefore confess your sins *to one another* . . . that you may be healed" (Jas. 5: 16). And "Bear *one another's* burdens, and so fulfill the law of Christ" (Gal. 6: 2). The italics are mine to emphasize that others are necessary so that we can honestly and adequately exteriorize our troubles and our rottenness by giving them words. That's what happens in counseling. How necessary this horizontal human dimension is, especially for the depressed person. God is not very real to someone who is depressed. He needs to confess his faults to another person, a real honest-to-goodness flesh and blood human being.

We need desperately in Protestantism to have some kind of reinstatement of the confessional, some means of making this whole dimension more a part of our practice. I am not arguing for the introduction of the confession as the Roman Catholic Church practices it, for that, too, is deficient from a psychological perspective. As it stands in Protestantism today, however, there are severe deficits in the practice of confession.

Probably the most severe problem is one of trust and identification. Bonhoeffer again says it well: "The final break through to fellowship does not occur, because, though they have fellowship with one another as believers and devout people, they do not have fellowship as the undevout and sinners. The pious fellowship permits no one to be a sinner. So everybody must conceal his sin from himself and from the fellowship. We dare not be sinners . . . so we remain alone with our sin, living in lies and hypocrisy. The fact is that we *are* sinners!" (p. 112, *Life Together*) And, I would add, the result is that emotional disorders, including depression, will be the inevitable consequences of such deceitful living.

Some of the old tent meetings of rural America in days gone by had a confessional of sorts. The open admission that came from public confession and the identification with the values of that body of believers to whom one confessed was quite functional. Everybody knew everybody else's business, so once someone had made such a confession that worked as a kind of control, many people monitored your life and helped you to prevent slip-ups and this increased your will power. This system has problems, too, however. Too often the body of believers failed to identify themselves as sinners. (As Alcoholics Anonymous members do.) Phariseeism had made such massive inroads that the confessing ones may have felt little identification with these already arrived types. Also, the excesses of this system made much of the practice offensive. It was often as ritualistic and as much a matter of role playing as the traditional Saturday night Catholic confessional.

193

Problems with Confession

Any practice of confession will have problems. Any good thing can be perverted. In fact, it seems that the more value there is to some idea or practice, the greater the likelihood that it will not only be perverted, but also counterfeited and misused. We will always have those who misuse the good for evil purposes—to gain power over others, to make money, to gain fame, to manipulate, to seduce, etc. The history of the church also tells us that far too many ministers and priests have been the lackeys of such perversity and misuse. I suppose because they deal in so many of the good things, the opportunity to misuse, as well as the possibility to cover misuse in righteous garb, is always a ready temptation for them. Anyway, confession is far too critical and important a dimension to leave in their hands. The Bible clearly tells us to make our confessions *to one another.*

Any practice of confession, however, can easily become ritualistic. That is a problem I have with the Roman Catholic confessional. Add to that the requirement that confession is obligatory rather than voluntary, and you really strip it of its psychological value. If anything must be spontaneous, self-initiated, and voluntary, it is confession of wrongdoing. Ritualizing confession emasculates it.

Another problem we face is that the honesty of confession can become cultic. This has already occurred in many circles today, especially with some secular pop psychology movements. Pharisaical demands to be open have become a new conformity, a new righteousness. Sin is being closed; righteousness is being open and readily expressing oneself. Many touchy-feely groups have gone this route. Exhibitionism is in; inhibitions are out. Unless we're willing to literally parade about in the psychic

194

nude, we are most unrighteous. The phariseeism that permeates many of these groups is disgusting. Their fundamental unwillingness to have assumptions challenged and to tolerate differences of opinion is a reverse moralism. We even find a pharisaical look-down-your-nose hierarchy of worth—"I'm more open than you," or "I've exposed more than you have," or "we've shared more marital problems than anyone in this group." Sick! This new priesthood of authenticity and openness has been no less capable of misuse and perversity than those medieval purveyors of dispensations of an older priesthood.

Another problem with confession is that for some it becomes a compulsion. The neurotic who tends to tell his troubles and story to anyone who will listen and thereby secures the attention he so desperately craves is one example. This kind of compulsive confessing accomplishes little or nothing. It is merely an attempt to gain sympathy or attention, often the *last* thing this person needs. By getting sympathy and attention, he fails to learn more appropriate and positive ways to go about getting these same needs met. Those for whom confession becomes a steady habit and a compulsion find others avoiding them. No one wants to listen to their endless repetition of misdeeds.

Such confession may also become a means of denying responsibility, a way to avoid dealing with what is really at issue. I've seen numerous clients who would incessantly confess some minute problem and repeat it over and over again and to many people. What was gnawing on their souls, however, was much more significant than the issue they were peddling all over the place. There was some really big, highly guilt-provoking behavior at stake. They were, you see, gaining some episodic relief by confessing and that's why it became compulsive. They were

195

gaining some of the psychological benefits of confession, but it wouldn't last and wasn't enough. We call this the red herring confession, the confession of some irrelevant or little issue as a means of avoiding the real one.

Still another problem with confession is that of selecting the persons to whom we dare confess. They should be people we know and trust, but the problem is we don't know just who we can trust. We should also be able to identify with those to whom we confess. If we know that these people, too, are sinners, it's much easier. One problem in the Christian church (as the Bonhoeffer quote so well portrays) is that the mechanics for acknowledgement of sinnerhood are just not there. Oh, at the abstract or theological level they are, but not at the psychological level.

How often I have asked clients, "Have you shared this with your minister or friends at church?" The almost universal response is, "You've got to be kidding. That's the *last* group of people I want to know this or would admit this to." How horribly sad! The place that supposedly exists for just this purpose has so perverted its existence that it has become the least used means of repentance, redemption, and restoration. What damage have these pharisees done? The church should be a hospital for sinners, not a country club or haven for saints. We must face the fact that in the twentieth century church we lack the mechanisms for such trust.

One more problem with confession is that it is highly contagious. The old camp meeting people knew that, so they frequently primed the pump. If you can get one confession going, you'll trigger others. This happens because so many of us are loaded with guilt of one kind or another and so ache to get it off our chests that we are ready candidates to join in if someone else will lead off. The impulsive nature of this kind of confession, however, makes it less than fully effective. It also makes for a lot of red herring confessions.

Conclusion

We have suggested in this chapter that confession will begin to solve the problem of depression which stems from real guilt. But what about other kinds of depression, especially those involving false guilt? Either way, confession is important, for only by getting the cards on the table, by stating what it is that we feel guilty for, can we differentiate between real and false guilt. We need to evacuate our soul to see ourselves and get at the causes and thus at the possible areas of our misery.

CHAPTER XI

COPING WITH DEPRESSION

MAKE NO MISTAKE, it is tough to cope with depression. The glut of popular books on the subject that suggest so many easy steps toward overcoming depression are not completely honest. Depression is such a multi-faceted and complex disorder, there is no one way to cure it. There is no set sequence of steps that if followed will succeed for everyone who suffers from depression.

I get angry at popular speakers and authors who make it all sound so easy. They do a disservice to those they intend to help. When a depression sufferer does not find relief after following a formula, he feels more guilty and inadequate than before. More feelings of having failed, of not achieving, of exerting himself unsuccessfully are piled on top of the already huge heap of bad feelings he already has.

Spiritual Boonswoggling

I especially get disturbed by those psycho-religious authors and speakers whose promises are totally out of proportion to the realities of depression and life. They suggest that if one will only get right with God, then depression will surely dissipate. They make it sound as though their particular set of steps have helped "count-

198

less thousands" of depressed persons. They cite case studies or refer to themselves as testimonials of the validity and effectiveness of their way of winning over depression. They also imply that if you come and attend their series of talks, listen to their cassettes, or read their literature, you will soon be on the way to health and happiness.

This approach is dishonest and deceitful. No one who has had long-term contact with depressed persons can maintain such simplistic approaches. That's why so many of these peddlers of perfect peace and constant happiness spend all their time running around the country telling others how to live. Close clinical contact over a long period of time with the ongoing problems of life does not allow the luxury of easy answerism. That is more easily maintained from the pulpit than the counseling room. I've had clients who have consulted with some big name popular types. In almost every case they were talked at and barely given opportunity to begin to set their problems out. Or they were reprimanded for not following the formula, and the speaker prescribed an additional dose of his latest book, cassette, or workshop. While they appeared to these clients as warm, effusive, and knowledgeable in the pulpit, they came on as cool, distant, and uncaring in a one-to-one relationship. It's easy, you see, to have answers in general; it is another to know what is best to do in the particular. The depressed person may get an instant high from his association with the "great man," but it lasts but a depressingly short time.

Real human existence and relationships are usually much more complex than the answers implied in the solutions of traveling salesmen. The realities of the lives of their hearers must therefore be kept at a distance. So must the realities and complexities of the speakers' own lives and relationships. Because they have often used themselves or their families as examples, they must care-

199

fully guard the distance of the real nitty-gritty of their own lives from others. Whereas the depressed person needs to count his successes, the manicy, super-enthusiastic evangelist needs to count his failures. In working with people we're more likely to learn more from our failures than from our successes. Failures for these purveyors of easy answers usually get chalked up to the uncooperativeness or unwillingness of the disturbed person or listener rather than to the faulty aspects of the plan. A successful plan is, of course, guaranteed in such an explanation of failures.

Cure Depends on Cause

Depression must never be handled in a simplistic way. We have suggested a number of different ways one can become depressed, and there are more ways than these. The solutions to overcome depression are somewhat dependent on how it came about in the first place. As we've already indicated, if you are depressed because you are failing to live up to your values, or are sinning, then it is quite likely that anti-depressive drugs will only provide temporary relief. Or if you are excessively dependent and passive, you are not likely to profit from a confession of waywardness. If you are lonely and depressed because your anger and hostility cuts you off from all those who get close to you, you are not likely to benefit from a period of rest or a vacation away.

Despite the similarity in the symptoms of depressed people, they're simply not alike in how they got that way, and it is not likely that everyone will get out of it by doing the same thing. The clinician's job is to delineate between the various kinds and causes of depression and to prescribe accordingly. This, however, is where the mental health field still lacks scientific certainty. We in psychology and psychiatry are at the same point here where the medical people were about 150 years ago with the understanding of fever. Fevers were then all lumped together without knowing whence they came. Now, however, we know there are many causes of high fever, and to go looking for one thing would be most foolhardy. They knew they had to reduce the fever, but unless they also treated the cause, the fever would likely return. Just so with depression. We must work immediately to reduce the depression, but if we don't find the cause, it will certainly return. (A depression which is biochemically caused is an exception here. Drugs may reduce the symptoms.)

Therapist's Task

The therapist must assess which route to depression each person has traveled. He needs to analyze the precipitating events as well as the features of the particular personality that may be predisposing or setting him up for depression. He must determine the degree to which ongoing stresses can be currently eliminated. The therapist needs to cut into the "giving up" process which eventuates in the ever-downward spiral of deeper and deeper depression. He needs to identify possible family interactions that reinforce or reward depressed behavior. He needs (as much as is possible and available to him) to help the client reinforce healthy behavior and eliminate secondary gain behavior. If he fails to do this, he will be limited in his ability to help this person, for the very behavior he wants to eliminate may be securing rewards and dividends that work against correction and cure. (If, for example, the therapist is attempting to build self-esteem, and parents or a spouse are tearing it down as quickly as it's being built up, the therapist may make few, if any gains.) The therapist also needs to aid the person in discovering and developing new habits to replace the depression-generating ones. This is the hardest part of therapy because habits are just that—habits. They have been long in the making, are highly entrenched, and difficult to break. New habits, too, will likely be long in the making. Even if things go well, it will take time before the new habits will be stronger than the old ones.

The therapist can't accomplish these tasks without the cooperation of the client. The client can do many things himself to alleviate the depression, and I intend in this chapter to enumerate some of the ways.

Depression is Self-Lifting

Before we do that, however, let's note the most hopeful and promising feature of depression. That is simply that depression is self-lifting. Given enough time things will correct themselves. The miserable feelings, the hopelessness, the agony of trying will all be left behind in a brighter tomorrow. Things *will* get better.

That fact is most reassuring, but there are some hazards to that. If, for example, the depressed person realizes that their misery will end eventually, it may be more difficult to enlist their cooperation in tasks which could hasten that end. There are also things they can do to keep it from getting worse.

We might ask why if it will eventually dissipate on its own, should we bother to get help? For one reason, it's important that they prevent the downward spiral of lethargy and lack of motivation. Many persons in a depressed state because of their feelings, do disastrous things such as quitting a job or leaving a marriage or letting a separated spouse gain custody of the children. Then they may regret these things when the depression lifts. It is also possible for them to reach the point of suicide. Besides this, who wants to continue in the misery and the hopelessness that attends depression? Perhaps we can't totally eliminate it, but we can modify it somewhat. Things *can* be done to keep depressed persons functioning and thus maintain whatever self-esteem they may have. Many tend to prolong their agony by their own natural reactions to their feelings. They can do something, however, about self-defeating behavior and shorten the time of their depression.

Depressions Are Not Always Avoidable

At the same time that we acknowledge that depressed moods eventually lift, we must also acknowledge that we can't always avoid them. There is an undulation to the moods of life which is quite natural and appropriate. We can't always be on top. Life has valleys, sin, sadness, etc. Every thoughtful person must face events that could precipitate depression. And every thoughtful person in touch with his own fallibilities must face up to the characteristics of his own personality and life that predispose him to difficulties and problems. At times depression is quite natural and even appropriate for all human beings.

As I write this, my wife lies in a hospital bed fighting a post-operative infection. She was taken to the hospital for emergency surgery just a few days ago. Her well-being and her ability to fight off this infection in her weakened state occupies all our thoughts. The second night she was in the hospital one of the children became ill and vomitted all over the place, as only children can do. The next morning I found that the lavatories in the house were clogged. Now add to that the fact that after visiting my wife in the hospital, and rushing home to attend to my children and clogged sewer lines, I was picked up and ticketed by the State Highway Patrol for doing sixty-two miles per hour on an interstate freeway with a fifty-five mile per hour limit. My wife's temperature was up again, and I had left her in a down state, and I was concentrating on everything else but my speed on that freeway. Preoccupied with legitimate concerns and the demanding responsibilities of the moment, I was, nonetheless, guilty. Some day I may look back upon this twenty-four hour fiasco and smile, maybe even laugh, but not now, I can assure you. It has all really been quite depressing. At this point I can only say, "Thank God for Liquid Plumber."

The passing of a loved one is certainly a depressing event, and it ought to be. That kind of loss of companionship, mutual affection, care, and concern is not met without suffering. That suffering will last for awhile, then come and go for awhile, but it will not instantly evaporate. The hole in our lives will remain for some time, and that is as it should be. (Only when acute grief becomes constant over an excessively long period of time, does it become an emotional problem.) So, there are times when being depressed is part of living. Those times will come as inevitably as the lifting of depressions.

Depression—God's Will

We must also acknowledge that God may intend for depression to come into our lives. Certainly, as we have previously indicated, the depression that follows violation of values is part of God's economy. Depressions which are not the result of sin could also be a part of God's will.

Many believe that the Lord permits His children to experience physical sickness or problems so as to accomplish something in someone's life. We all feel that some adversity can produce growth in our lives. Why not emotional problems, as well, even depression?

In a very familiar biblical passage we read that "we rejoice in our sufferings, knowing that suffering produces endurance, and endurance produces character, and character produces hope . . ." (Rom. 5:3). That sequence that ends in hope is the same sequence that is psychologically so important for children in learning how to cope with problems. We might like it otherwise, but we simply can't place hope earlier in the sequence. Endurance and character may be essential to hope, and we work on that sequence in therapy.

Martin Luther is a good example of this. His depressions resulted in important building blocks in his life which in turn resulted in changes in the very foundation of western civilization itself. Who can say that these depressions of Martin Luther's were not productive?

I have read somewhere that William Cowper's famous hymn, "God Moves in a Mysterious Way His Wonders to Perform," was written during deep depression, even approaching suicide. One verse in that song goes:

> Ye fearful saints, fresh courage take;
>   The clouds ye so much dread
> Are big with mercy and will break
>   In blessings on your head.

God may have a purpose in the depressions we experience. They can, in fact, teach us volumes. Right now, with fears of loss of my wife because of her seeming inability to fight off this post-operative infection, I have become acutely aware once again of all she means to me and to this household. Without her presence a massive cavity would exist in our lives. (I have also come to appreciate immensely the tasks that she performs in this family.)

Perhaps God intends depression to teach us that certain aspects of our lives or personalities need changing. Our dependencies, insecurities, inferiority feelings, or hostilities may need to be dealt with more profitably than we have in the past. Depression may be the inevitable outcome of inappropriate lifestyles which need correction. Perhaps the natural laws of God's universe are playing themselves out in our lives, and depression reminds us that we need to realign our lives.

Act Yourself Out of Depression

If you want to get yourself out of the slough of depression, *act* your way out. Now I'm sure that sounds like strange and simplistic advice. But it works. There are actions, simple actions, that can begin to remove, inch by inch, that burdensome boulder that bears so heavily on your emotions. E. Stanley Jones once said, "It is easier to *act* yourself into a new way of thinking than to *think* your way into a new way of acting."

Such a notion will strike many as getting the cart before the horse. Certainly it will seem that way to many depressed people. They'll say, "but that's just it, I don't *feel* like doing that." Or, "I don't think it will do any good." But it does. An increasingly large body of evidence in social psychology suggests that if you want to change attitudes, you don't so much go at it by changing people's thoughts. Instead, you change their actions. Once they act in certain ways, the thoughts will change accordingly. You change attitudes by changing actions.

I've seen patients buoyed up simply because someone insisted that they go for a walk or to a movie or out to eat or to a party with them. Oh, they didn't feel like going and they had fears (of interacting with others, of "being seen like this," etc.), and it wasn't as good an experience as it would have been had they not been depressed, but it still helped. At times therapists prescribe such activities. For example, each day you will take a walk in the morning at 10:30. Carry on some outside activity every Friday or Saturday evening. Work on this or that project at home for so long each day, etc.

A number of recent research studies on depression support this notion. They have found it helpful to get patients doing tasks, even simple ones such as card-sorting, tasks at which the person can't fail. Then as they successfully accomplish these tasks, they're moved up to higher, more difficult tasks. These graded task assignments allow the depressed person to act his way up to do things he was convinced he couldn't do.

For one thing these graded task assignments help to relieve depression by convincing the patient that he can do it. He views his own performance and has to acknowledge what he has done. It also gives him a feeling of efficacy, something that he lacks at the moment. At the same time it forces him to focus on something other than his misery and the automatic negative thoughts that dominate his thinking.

Martin Luther made the following observation about his own negative thoughts and depression: "When I am assailed with heavy tribulation, I rush out amongst my pigs rather than remain alone by myself. The human heart, unless it be occupied with some employment, leaves space for the Devil, who wiggles himself in and brings with him a whole host of evil thoughts, temptations, and tribulations which grind out the heart."

The depressed person often claims that he just can't do things very well, that his thinking is all confused, and that he can't remember things well. He fears he'll mess up whatever he touches. Interestingly enough, recent research indicates that depressed persons function as well as they normally do on thinking tasks. He may feel as though he isn't doing as well, but that's only a feeling. I've heard depressed clients complain that they are just not doing such and such a task well. When I asked how their bosses or supervisors felt, I found little or no complaint. The boss may complain that the person *talks* so much about how badly he is doing, but he has no complaints about the performance itself.

Act Out by Moving Out

Avoid being alone. Depressed people naturally tend to withdraw into themselves and stay away from others. They go to bed or retreat to their room or grab a six-pack and go off by themselves to drink it. Or they find a corner and cry or write down all their bad feelings in a diary or rehearse past failures endlessly to themselves. Rather than work so hard to be alone, they could help themselves by seeking out people or situations which involve joy and companionship. Getting together with others will give them a more realistic perspective on their problems. Consulting with others helps them avoid making mountains out of mole hills. Seeing other people who are not overwhelmed by their stress can be reassuring. Withdrawing, on the other hand, means trying to do it alone, trying to pull ourselves up by our own bootstraps, and we get trapped in the quicksand of our own depressed feelings.

Act Out by Helping Out

Help someone else. Few things will alleviate depression any quicker than finding someone more needy than you are and helping them. Of course, you respond, "How can I help anyone with the shape I'm in?" Well, you can, and nothing can bend you out of that shape more than seeing and doing something for someone who's in worse shape than you are.

When a person with a headache or a bad back attends to someone with cancer, it is amazing how insignificant that bad back or headache seems. I've seen this dynamic happen repeatedly in group therapy sessions. Frequently someone comes out of the group saying, "Wow, my problems seem like peanuts compared to his." One of the significant benefits of group therapy is just this, that hurting and needy persons are caught up in helping other needy and hurting persons. They profit from the aid and support they give others. Their own feelings of worth and value increase as a result.

We find the principle that works here written in Scripture: "He who finds his life will lose it, and he who loses his life for my sake will find it" (Matt. 10:39). When we focus on ourselves, we really lose ourselves. This is one problem I have with some of the current self-exploration, navel-contemplating, meditation fads. What happens when you don't like what you see inside? In Job we read of an intriguing turn of emotional events, "The Lord turned the captivity of Job when he prayed for his friends" (Job 42:10). One way out of the captivity of depression is by turning to others.

How ironic this is when you think about it. So many depressed persons do not feel needed or wanted. They feel dependent on others, and they feel others don't need or want them. They don't feel of worth or value to themselves, because they don't feel of worth and value to others. They are often highly concerned with rejection or the fact that they don't feel loved. Some may even *demand* love, recognition, and concern from others or manipulate others into giving it to them.

Serving others in need could meet all these needs for

the depressed person—unneeded, unrecognized, un-wanted, not of worth and value. Serving others in need will, more than anything else make you feel needed, wanted, and worthy. Work on loving others rather than working so hard on securing their love, and you may directly meet your own needs. Then you will no longer need to prove yourself worthy of love and acceptance.

The person who wants to feel needed will find a vast resource in the elderly in our society who would give anything to have a repeat visitor, a helping hand, a little companionship, a trip out, or a shoulder to cry on. That, of course, is only one segment of society in need. Maybe, just maybe, those who don't feel needed, haven't made themselves needed. If so, it is certainly not for lack of need.

Act Out by Getting Out

Some intriguing suggestions for therapy have come out of the model which we called "Learned Helpless-ness." The idea here is that many persons have learned to be helpless, and this helplessness interferes with any future attempts to help themselves.

Depressed persons believe they are helpless in achiev-ing the rewards they want in life or avoiding the punish-ment they don't want. As a result, they don't try. The goal, then, is to get them to learn that they can be effec-tive in getting what they want, or avoiding what they don't want, by using their own resources.

One group of researchers placed depressed persons in what they called an anti-depression room and insulted them until they became angry. They reprimanded them, for example, for the way they did some simple task. At the moment the person became angry or asserted him-self, the researchers apologized to him and released him.

Strange as it may seem, the depression improved with such treatment.

The key to this, obviously, is action, moving out, doing something. Feelings and attitudes then follow the behavior. Act as though you feel differently and you will.

Positive Focus

A popular song from my younger days began:

Accentuate the positive;
Eliminate the negative;
Latch onto the affirmative.

At that time Norman Vincent Peale wrote the bestseller, *The Power of Positive Thinking*. More recently a widely sold book entitled *I'm O.K., You're O.K.* has gained great popularity. We could cite other examples. In every age, it seems, this theme of positive focus recurs. At first glance this seems shallow advice for someone struggling with depression. Telling them to think positively is not particularly profound. However, the Bible tells us that "as he thinketh in his heart, so is he" (Prov. 23: 7). In Philippians we are told "Whatever is true, whatever is honorable, whatever is just, whatever is pure, whatever is lovely, whatever is gracious, if there is any excellence, if there is anything worthy of praise, think about these things" (Phil. 4: 8).

The psychology of all this is clear. The imagination of man is a powerful force in his life. The images in our minds influence our behavior and our feelings. If we dwell on the negatives—real and imagined rejections, the losses of life, the distressing happenings—we can all work ourselves into depression. If we ruminate on all our past failures, inadequacies and misfortunes, we will all

211

soon be candidates for suicide. Luckily, most of us maintain our ambivalence here in our imagination as we do elsewhere in our lives. We temper our memory of losses by remembering our gains as well. The depressed person doesn't do this. He rehashes the negative over and over again. No wonder he experiences depression.

To alleviate depression we must first break into this vicious circle of negativism. Then we must replace the negative thoughts. Many persons struggle to rid themselves of negative thoughts, but they fail miserably. They fail to see that you can't remove one focus from your mind unless you fill it with something else. You cannot *not* think. You can't make your mind go blank. We use the phrase, but actually it's impossible. The brain works constantly. Our mind is always full of thoughts, even when we're sleeping. We can't control that, but we *can* control the focus of our thoughts. Remember the Bible story about sweeping the house clean of one devil, just to have it replaced by seven more? It's the same with trying to get rid of negative thoughts. Unless you also control what goes into your head to replace those negative thoughts, you won't be successful.

We must first of all identify our depression-generating thoughts, especially those automatic negative phrases we keep saying over and over. For example, "I just don't have what it takes, I guess," or "I'm not able to do that," or "I wish I could be like others," or "Why did this have to happen to me," or blame-placing on our parents or spouses. In therapy we will often point out the distortion of reality these negative thoughts involve. We will also review and check the observations on which these negative thoughts and phrases are based. This usually allows us to get some objectivity and distance from these depression-generating notions. Then we try to neutralize these negative thoughts by having the depressed per-

212

son recite reasons why that thought is invalid.

The depressed person must learn that it is not frustration and conflict which depress him, but *how he reacts* to frustration and conflict. A famous Greek thinker, Epictetus, put it this way: "Men are not disturbed by things, but by the views which they take of them."

The Apostle Paul understood this. He told us that "You also must consider yourselves dead to sin and alive to God in Christ Jesus" (Rom. 6:11). And he wrote ". . . sin will have no dominion over you, since you are not under law but under grace" (Rom. 6:14). Is he saying that sin can no longer have an effect on the Christian? No, he's saying that the Christian has a new focus, the positive focus of grace rather than the negative focus of the law. Therefore, sin need not maintain such control over his life. He can consider himself out from under its control. It's the same with the negative "I can't" or "I'm not capable, or able" of depressed persons. Such negatives only lead to despair, to hopelessness, to feelings of being trapped and helpless. Through the grace of God we can alter the mental image we have of ourselves. We are forgiven rather than damned. We are then, Paul tells us, to "put on Christ."

The depressed person needs to change his self-talk. Those who suffer from low self-esteem find it difficult to maintain a positive image. They need to realize that this image is built up of the momentary evaluations they make of themselves. Overall self-esteem is the accumulative effect of all the bits of self-talk that go on. If we continually make disparaging remarks about ourselves, these become a self-fulfilling prophecy. We can't live with constant criticism, even from ourselves, without it taking its toll.

The Christian especially should be able to cut into this vicious circle of negative self-talk. Knowing that God

213

accepts him, and considers him of worth and value, he can no longer with integrity, bad-mouth himself. He has a basis of self-acceptance that the non-Christian may not enjoy.

We can't alter overall self-esteem, however, without altering the momentary evaluations that go to make it up. It may help to keep a record, sort of a diary, of positive self-statements or make up lists of things for which you are grateful. Carry this list with you and review it a number of times through the day. Talk aloud to yourself. Say the positive thought out loud. Repeat it. Write it down. Coddle it. Reward yourself for positive thoughts. Eat something you like, a dish of ice cream, a cookie, after you've thought five positive thoughts about yourself. But *never* reward yourself for feeling miserable or having depressed thoughts. You'd be amazed how many people reward themselves (especially with food) for their bad feelings. Unwittingly they are rewarding their own depressed behavior and that's the way both good and bad habits are learned.

At the same time, don't let negative thoughts go unchallenged. Argue with yourself. Don't let a negative thought cross your mind without also adding a positive thought to it. "Yes I know that I'm not an especially outgoing type of person, but it's also true that I am a very reliable person." "Maybe it's true that I lack financial assets, but I have a sensitive spirit." Maintain that ambivalence toward yourself that is realistic.

Christian Resources For Depression

We have already alluded to resources that the Christian has available to him to cope with depression. Let's spell out several more.

The most significant Christian resource of all is the

acceptance and love of God. The feeling of being of worth and value is not something anyone can do for himself. It must come from without. Most of us as small children experienced the unconditional love of our parents and families. Because others loved us and considered us to be of worth and value, we learned to love ourselves. As I said before, I think God made toddlers cute and attractive because at that age they need that foundation of love, affection, and acceptance. Without it they can spend a lifetime of self-hatred, self-depreciation, and self-rejection. This is what has happened to many neurotics. They don't feel acceptable to themselves or to others. Thus they try to compensate for this by all kinds of neurotic tricks, but you can't trick or deceive others into accepting you.

Many children receive only conditional love—"Shape up and I'll love you." That, of course, will leave a person feeling acceptable only when he measures up. Conditional love is certainly an important dimension in growing up and in family relationships, but conditional love will *only* work when there is already a firm base from unconditional love from early life.

What about the poor soul who has no base of unconditional love? Is he doomed to a neurotic search to find it somewhere? Here the genius of the Christian message is unparalleled good news. God loves us. Even while we are quite unacceptable, God loves us. Love *must* come from without, and for the Christian that has happened *regardless* of how wretched his family background has been, *regardless* of the deprivations of love that he has known, *regardless* of his lack of self-love and acceptance. The vicious circle of being unloved which leads to self-depreciation and rejection, which in turn leads to depression, has been broken. For "while we were yet sinners Christ died for us" (Rom. 5:8). Frequently in therapy the vicious circle is broken. I've seen it also happen through a marriage or a friendship. (I've also seen marriages and friendships contracted to *make* that happen, later to turn quite sour when it doesn't.)

Then, too, our capacity to love is contingent on our having first been loved. To love others, we must have first experienced love ourselves. This is the reason why the typical juvenile delinquent can be such a hateful person, so seemingly incapable of loving others. Often he has not been loved himself, or only conditionally loved. Our ability to love God is not based within ourselves but comes as a result of His love for us. "We love, because he first loved us" (I John 4:19).

This is the sequence of justification and sanctification in our lives. Justification is unconditional. We can't do one thing to earn salvation, i.e., acceptance with God. It comes from God's unmerited favor, His grace alone. But sanctification is a different story. God wants us to shape up, and we can *because* we have that foundation of unconditional love on which to base our efforts. Like the child who can exert himself to achieve if he has that base of love from early life, we, because of God's grace, can go out and love others. Knowing God's love can become that foundation for anyone who wants it.

Resting in the Sovereignty of God

I really like that phrase, "resting in the sovereignty of God," but what in the world does that mean to a person in the depth of depression? The sovereignty of God simply means that God is in charge. He is running the universe. The drama of human existence is under His direction. Not only did He create this universe, He maintains it, and my own little universe is part of His. He's the director of the total drama, and He knows the final act.

216

If God is in charge of this world, my world, then whether I shall be anxious and in dread, or at rest and ease will depend on what He is like. That, of course, we already know. God is like Jesus. That's one reason Christ came into this world, to show us what God was like. God is a Father who unconditionally loves and cares for His creation. Yet He cares so much that He doesn't impose Himself on us. He gives us an independent identity. We can choose for ourselves how we wish to respond to Him. This God is like the Father in the prodigal son story. The prodigal son, though made and shaped by his Father and given an inheritance (apparently unconditional), was free to do as he wished. He was free to fail if he wished, and he did. But in the depths of his depression (a depression of real guilt and sin), he "came to himself" and reflected on what his father was like. Then he realized that no matter how he had botched it, his father was the kind of person to whom he could return.

God is like that, and that's why we can rest in His sovereign control. In John we read, "In the world you have tribulation; but be of good cheer, I have overcome the world" (John 16:33).

The psalmist directly approaches depression with this same resource: "Why are you cast down, O my soul, and why are you disquieted within me? Hope in God" (Ps. 43:5). The hope of the Christian is in God. Thus he is *never* without hope.

In the passage from John, we may easily miss something because of the meaning the word "tribulation" has to us. Actually the original meaning of this word is much more directed to emotions than to calamity. The translation might better include the concept of being anxious, pressured, or trapped. In this world we have pressures and anxieties, but God has overcome all of these. Not only that, but "God is our refuge and strength, a very

217

present help in trouble" (Ps. 46:1). (Italics mine.) God is not only in control, but He is with us. If this is what God is really like, then most assuredly we can rest in His sovereignty.

Give some thought to what God is like. Rehearse His attributes and the history of His dealings with man. Again the Psalmist tells us how, "My soul is cast down within me, I remember thee from the land of Jordan" (Ps. 42:6). "My flesh and my heart may fail, but God is the strength of my heart and my portion for ever" (Ps. 73:26). God does not expect us to understand the relationship between His sovereignty and this world's happenings, but He does expect us to trust Him.

Music as Therapy

Many depressed persons find solace in music. The order and harmony of music transfers to the disordered and chaotic world of the depressed person. It can have a soothing and calming effect, an ordering effect.

Making music yourself is better still. If you play an instrument, get it out and try to bring forth some sequential order and melody out of it. It may be hard to get started, but it will lift your spirit. Play some each day. If all you have is a voice for music, use it. Push yourself. Get an old songbook and go through those old familiar numbers. Sing aloud.

I envy those who have musical skills. They can produce harmony in their lives and a lifting of their spirits that others can't. I've noticed how often my wife, when she's feeling down for some reason, will sit down at the piano. After fifteen or twenty minutes she'll come away feeling more peaceful, more together, more collected, more serene. And it lifts my spirits, as well, just to listen to her music.

Physical Exercise

Physical exercise is essential to our modern lives, especially our emotional lives. We live stepped up existences, but we never really get physical release from all that stimulation and arousal. We accumulate all kinds of tension as we move through the day. Our muscles get tight, and our blood pressure goes up.

This is even more true for the depressed or neurotic person. They are easily aroused emotionally, quick to become tense, easily threatened. Their bodies tighten like a drum and they become exhausted from all this conflict.

When we're tense or when our minds are tumbling with all sorts of threats and stress, we can't sleep. The next day we can't mobilize sufficient energy to fight the struggles and deal with the conflicts. So we live in a semi-exhausted state all the time—fatigued, even exhausted, but too tense to sleep well. Again, we have one of those vicious circles that leads to depression.

Time and again I've suggested some daily physical exercise for such people (with permission from their physician) and have seen the vicious circle of exhaustion broken, even when the basic problems have not yet been remedied. Because they use up some of this nervous energy and tension in physical exercise, they can at least get some sleep, which in turn allows them to mobilize themselves to confront their problems with greater vigor and stamina.

Nothing can substitute for the therapy of physical exercise. I've found it very helpful in my own fast-paced life. Counseling with hurting people can itself be very emotionally draining. And working with some potential suicidal cases keeps me very much on edge, especially after a middle-of-the-night frantic call. I find that when

I've exercised physically, I can sleep better after that kind of arousal.

Actually, I think physical exercise may help us more emotionally than physically. (I have some friends in the medical and physical education field who won't deny that.) But I suppose such an argument borders on the ridiculous. Obviously, it's beneficial for the whole person—body, soul, and spirit.

Drug Therapy

I'm not a medical person, so I am not qualified to evaluate drugs in treating depression. I can, however, make some observations regarding what I've seen. Certainly, when depression is endogenous in nature, i.e., caused by possible biochemical imbalances or physiological disturbance, drug therapy can be appropriate. Don't let my comments in chapter eight regarding the dulling of the sense of conviction of sin mislead you into thinking that I believe it is never appropriate.

There are also times when drug therapy is helpful in making psychotherapy and counseling possible. People can be so withdrawn or so hyper they need medication so that they can begin to converse effectively about their problems. Medication can also ameliorate depression enough so that a person can continue to work, avoid hospitalization, or prevent suicide.

Nonetheless, I am concerned with what appears to be the promiscuous use of chemotherapy (the use of drugs to cope with emotional stress). Drugs don't deal with psychological causes. Those causes may still exist when the drugs are removed and the vicious cycle is liable to repeat itself all over again. Too often I've seen clients who had taken mood altering drugs, but the causes for those moods had gone undealt with. Physicians have so little time to deal with these more remote emotional causes that it is easy to bypass them. It's not the doctor's fault for not considering such causes. I've seen many, many clients who simply haven't told the doctor the nature of their emotional distress. They might admit to "being tense," or "pressured," or "under a lot of strain," but they haven't delivered the sources of that distress to their doctors. Sometimes, too, the patients haven't connected in their own minds their tension and the events in their lives producing those tensions.

Another hazard to drug treatment is that often individuals so treated will conclude that their depression is a physically induced illness and thereby relieve themselves of any responsibility for their disorder. As a result, they may fail to change or reorder their lives or their situation so as to make possible their chances of total or ultimate recovery. They may then need the pills as a constant crutch forever.

Shock Treatments

As with drug therapy, electric shock treatment is a medical treatment and is out of my domain. I have studied the research on it extensively, however, and there are no conclusive answers to it. Shock treatment remains controversial. Some psychiatrists I know will not administer it at all; others are enthusiastic about it.

It is, however, with depression that electroconvulsive shock therapy has been most effective. It is most often used when a patient is severely suicidal or if he doesn't respond to anti-depressive medications. Usually, only the more severe depressions are treated with electroconvulsive shock. Progress may also be quicker with shock therapy than with other forms of intervention for such severely depressed cases. Since the introduction of vari-

221

ous anti-depressant drugs, shock treatment has played a decreasing role in the treatment of depression.

Spontaneous Recovery

Finally let me mention the concept of spontaneous recovery. By this we mean that when we're working to rid ourselves of habits we don't want, given the passage of time those habits will return momentarily. You think they've been absolutely licked, but here they are back again, seemingly as automatic as ever. The important thing, however, is that they will be there only *momentarily*. Don't give up at this point. Don't give in. Habits wear off more than they drop off. Keep at it. Don't be defeated by the momentary intrusion of old ways of behaving.

Because so many of the therapeutic changes that are helpful to the depressed person are really changes in habit, dropping old habits and building new ones, this spontaneous recovery concept is important to understand. We can expect it when we're learning new habits. And it will come when we least expect it. That in itself may be disheartening, but it doesn't mean that all our work has been in vain or useless. It happens without our ever being aware of it. Habits are automatic behaviors. Until your new behavior pattern is as automatic as the old habit, expect periodic returns and intrusions. But don't let it get you down. The new habit can become just as automatic and just as powerful as the old one if you'll stick with it.

CONCLUSION

BEFORE WE CONCLUDE our discussion, we must refer to some aspects of depression we haven't mentioned. We've focused on the psychology of depression and have not talked about the biology or sociology of depression. This is not to say that these aspects of depression are not important or critical. They are. Though neither of these areas are readily apparent in the experience of depression, either or both of these areas may very well be basic to the causes of depression. The very fact that women appear to struggle with depression more than men may, for example, be due to physiological or sociological factors.

A vast amount of research goes on in these areas with many biochemical, genetic, and neurological theories of depression. While the research into these theories has not determined nor concluded very much, some of the findings are worth considering. For example, it appears that changes or deficits of certain neurotransmitter substances in the brain relate to depression in one form or another. Researchers have found deficits of amines at specific sites in the brain as well as low levels of catecholamine and a low supply of norepinephrine. Neurological theories have suggested malfunction of a specific part of the brain such as the hypothalamus (an area having to do with many of man's motivational functions). Some research has suggested that some people may have a "biological predisposition" such that they may respond to stress with depression more readily than would most people. Some researchers suggest that genetic factors influence depression.

None of these theories or findings seem relevant to all forms of depression. The depressive disorder that appears to have shown the most biochemical or genetic relationships has been the manic-depressive disorder. Here again we must remember that depression is not one thing; there are different kinds of depression and it can take many forms. It is most unlikely, therefore, that any single factor will be isolated as *the* cause of depression. We would expect, however, the so-called endogenous depressions (no apparent outside cause) to be the most likely ones to have biochemical, genetic, or neurological factors as causes.

Concern with hypoglycemia has been a recent rage in our nation with medical opinion divided on its significance. Some suggest that this problem has definite implications for the emotional life of the person affected. Chronic fatigue experienced by the sufferer of hypoglycemia would be obviously related to such a disorder, and is also a component of depression. The suggestion here is that nutrition may be a factor in certain emotional disorders. The ability to metabolize certain substances may be faulty and diet may need to be controlled. This, of course, is a biological explanation of depression. I am not competent to make judgments here, but I have been impressed with some neurotics who seemed extremely eager to jump on the hypoglycemia bandwagon when it came along. I saw some who were so insistent that this was a disorder from which they suffered, that they persisted to believe so even though they had consulted four or five physicians who insisted otherwise. It provided them with a biological explanation for their symptoms and as a result removed them from feelings of responsibility for their emotional distress. Biological causes of emotional problems apparently have less stigma than psychological causes. It is somehow easier to say I have a mixed-up metabolism mechanism, than to say I have trouble living with aspects of my personality or trouble living successfully with others. Hypoglycemia, however, is not the only physical disorder used in this way. Almost any physical disorder (real or imagined) can be used by a person to explain or rationalize to himself his emotional distress.

Whenever we discuss the cause of a disorder, we run the risk of making an either/or problem out of it—e.g. either biological or psychological factors cause depression; if it is one then it cannot be the other. Either/or thinking usually tends to be overly simplistic and that is certainly the case here.

For some reason many people assume that emotion refers to something non-physical, something "in our heads." Nothing could be further from the truth. Emotional activities are *always* accompanied by changes in the central nervous system or the autonomic nervous system, our physical bodies. We could say the same about the word "psychological." When some people learn they have a psychogenic (psychologically caused) problem, they assume they have nothing physically wrong. Again this is mistaken thinking. If, for example, you have an ulcer that is psychogenic in origin, you *do* have an ulcer. It exists in your stomach.

We can't separate man into biological, psychological, and spiritual parts just to account for some particular disorder. We have another chicken and egg problem whenever we attempt to account for one aspect by the other. Biochemical abnormality may be the product of experience, and experience may be the product of biochemical abnormality. Researchers found, for example, that animals made to become depressed or helpless, showed changes in their brain chemistry. We will never understand depression by adopting any unifaceted approach. Both biological and psychological causes interact with one another so that we can't easily ascertain which precedes or causes the other.

We can say the same about sociological factors in depression. We have found cultural differences in the occurrence of depression from one society or culture to another, also from one sub-cultural group to another.

Primitive societies appear to have less depression than civilized societies. Some reports suggest a low frequency of depression in Africa, at least in the Africa of ten or twenty years ago. Depression has also been found to occur less with southern blacks than with both whites and northern blacks. Suicide is also reported to be less for them. The suggestion has been made that this may be due to the very low expectation and aspiration levels of southern blacks.

People whose vocations uproot them every few months or years report a higher frequency of depression. This has sometimes been called the "Cape Kennedy Syndrome." The mobile engineer or executive who is forced by his company to move himself and his family every few years seems to set his wife up for depression. This leads us to think that possibly the increasing rootlessness of our society may be a reason for the increase in depression. Rootlessness creates an intimacy vacuum. As a result people live not only more anonymously, but also a more lonely and even a more secretive life. They have fewer significant others' shoulders to cry on or people to whom they can open their lives.

Depression has also been reported to be high with

youth associated with the protest movements of the late sixties and early seventies. To go to another extreme, researchers found a high rate of depression (compared to other emotional disorders) with the Hutterites, an exclusive pietistic, separatist group. Both groups likely have aspirations that make expectations seldom realized.

We could go on, but that is really the job of someone other than a psychologist. I have made these few references and observations in the biological and sociological areas merely to point out that they exist and that a purely psychological approach is incomplete without them.

Suicide is another large topic relating to depression that we have not covered in this book. Depressed persons make up a significant proportion of the people who commit suicide. One of the best arguments for getting help and not sitting around and waiting for the depression to lift (even though it will), is just that—the frequency of depression in suicide cases. Many persons who would not otherwise give a second thought to suicide as a way out of their problems may do so when deeply depressed. Once that depression has lifted, they wonder how they could possibly have thought about doing away with themselves. The incidence of depression is one of the best arguments for suicide prevention and crises centers.

Finally, this leads me to say what must be obvious by now. If you're depressed, go talk to someone about it—your pastor, a trusted friend, your spouse, and see if you can evacuate yourself of these bad feelings. If that doesn't work, seek professional help. By all means possible, cut into those vicious circles we have discussed that drag you deeper and deeper into the slough of despond. It can be done. "For God hath not given us the spirit of fear; but of power, and of love, and of a sound mind" (II Tim. 1:7).